OPIUM KINGS of OLD HAWAII

OPIUM KINGS of OLD HAWAII

JOHN MADINGER

Published by The History Press
Charleston, SC
www.historypress.com

First published 2021

Manufactured in the United States

ISBN 9781467147118

Library of Congress Control Number: 2021931211

CONTENTS

Contents

INTRODUCTION

The war was over. The Great War, the War to End All Wars, the War that Would Make the World Safe for Democracy ground to a bloody and exhausted close earlier that day. All across the earth, the word went out, traveling by telegraph and wireless so that the celebrations could begin, even in the remotest corners of a planet that had just seen its very first world war. At eleven o'clock that morning in France and Belgium, the guns of the western front fell silent for the first time in four years, and from Europe's capitals to the heart of Africa, men turned away from killing. In San Francisco that day, thirty thousand people came out to celebrate in the streets. All of them wore gauze masks, the scantest protection against the flu pandemic that would kill forty or fifty million around the world before it burned itself out.

At the far end of the earth, on treeless, windswept Akutan Island, Alaska Territory, the winter crew at the North Pacific Sea Products plant gathered for lunch and celebrated the armistice. Most of the company's fleet had left Akutan for winter quarters in Seattle or Tacoma. Facing the ferocious storms and monstrous seas of the Gulf of Alaska and the Bering Sea in winter, the whaling and fishing seasons were over, and the North Pacific men could relax in the ragged collection of buildings that huddled at the edge of the harbor as they waited for the short November day to end. Outside, the wind began to pick up, whistling past the oil tanks ashore and onto the bay, where a tired little schooner rode at anchor in the light, choppy waves.

Pacific Yacht Club, Sausalito, 1882, *Halcyon*'s first home. *California History Room, California State Library.*

The main building warmed beautifully, with two stoves going as the men inside talked about the armistice, the end of the remote threat that the war had posed to their isolated little world. They talked business—their business of killing. The year had been the most successful in the company's history with 310 whales taken and construction workers coming from Seattle to expand the plant at Akutan to handle the extra load. All of the construction men were gone and the crews from the whaling ships, too, leaving just the skeleton staff for the whaling station and the schooner offshore, men who had a long, cold, dreary winter ahead of them, one that promised to start up shortly. The barometer in the office dropped, and the wind outside continued to rise.

Not all of the men would be there in the spring. The great Spanish flu pandemic ravaged Alaska that fall and winter, wiping out some villages, blasting entire Aleut communities into eternity and orphaning thousands of children. Even as the men of Akutan celebrated peace over their dinner, the steamer SS *Victoria* passed through the Aleutians on its way from Nome to Seattle. It had 700 passengers aboard. By the time it docked, 135 had come down with the flu, and 31 were dead.

Because of its isolation, Akutan wouldn't feel the flu until May, when the disease killed mostly older women and children from the small Aleut settlement on the island. Still, some of those around the table that afternoon, big, hearty Norwegians or brash American sailormen, all in the twenty-five to thirty-five age bracket that this reaper coveted, would be buried by June in the little cemetery up the hill. The flu took fourteen from Akutan and forty-four from Dutch Harbor and Unalaska, the next island to the west, and it would have been much worse if the navy and the coast guard hadn't put doctors and working parties of sailors with rations and medical aid ashore. All of that was in the future; today, the wind began to batter the buildings with snow, and it moaned in the rigging of the schooner.

In the warm hut where the men gathered for dinner, the winds rattled the walls as the darkness closed in, shutting out the world outside, hiding the gray hills around the harbor and the little ship now riding at double anchors against the storm. Nobody was aboard the schooner this evening. There were no witnesses to its final trial. It had been born a racing yacht, built to capture the attention of everyone who saw it on the more placid waters of San Francisco Bay. Tonight, as the storm raged and the crew celebrated, it was all alone. But it was not forgotten nor ever would be.

Halcyon was a legend.

1
SEA WITCH

THE ENCHANTING *HALCYON*

Jack London knew the ship years later. Still beautiful and still an enchantress, by that time, it had settled into a darker and bloodier career off Japan and in the Bering Sea. By 1893, they called it the *Halcyon* no more, but the sailormen of the Pacific all remembered it from the legend. So did the crew of the *Sophia Sutherland*, a sealing schooner that took young Jack to Japan for skins that year. In time, London would leave the sea, settle down and write tales of adventure and danger, of romantic South Seas Islands and frozen Arctic wastes. He wrote of the sea, too, and over the years, with the memory still haunting him, he wrote five times of *Halcyon* or the opium ring that sailed it. In a 1919 story, he said of *Halcyon*, "She was an opium smuggler and she sailed like a witch." Yes, the old ship still had the power to captivate; even after all that time, the celebrity and the myth followed it.

Halcyon was born a star, coming into the world as the ultimate plaything, a racing yacht for a millionaire's son. Harry Tevis commissioned it in 1882 for the races and regattas of San Francisco Bay's yacht club scene. Tevis, studying to be a medical doctor at the University of California that year, was the son of Lloyd Tevis, 49er, mogul in mining and banking and president of both the Wells Fargo Express Company and the Southern Pacific Railroad. Yachting was popular with the smart set at the time, with three clubs dividing the yachts of the area, and Tevis sailed his schooner, *White Wing*, under the flag of the elite Pacific Yacht Club (PYC). Headquartered across the Golden Gate in Sausalito, the PYC was home to some of San Francisco's wealthiest yacht owners and the largest of the boats on the bay.

Schooner *Halcyon* on San Francisco Bay, August 15, 1886. *William Letts Oliver Collection, University of California, Berkeley.*

Halcyon's cost prompted some wild speculation in the yachting community. One high-end rumor had Tevis shelling out a cool $120,000, a lot of money in 1883, especially for someone not yet out of medical school and with no fortune of his own. Comparable yachts went for $20,000 or $30,000 at the time, and several years later, the builder quoted *Halcyon*'s price at a much more reasonable $25,000 ($682,500 in 2020 dollars).

Although the newspapers long afterward reported that *Halcyon* was born in the Benicia shipyard of legendary shipbuilder Matthew Turner, this was an understandable mistake. Turner, whose yards launched more wooden sailing vessels than any other American builder, had a reputation for constructing fine, fast, sturdy ships. He also created beautiful ones. Turner put *Halcyon*'s racing rival, the Spreckels Brothers' $22,000 *Lurline* into the water the same year, and people widely regarded it as one of the handsomest boats on the bay, but he couldn't take credit for Tevis's new toy.

That credit went to the "modeler" Winslow G. Hall and to shipbuilder William Isaac Stone. *Halcyon* was part of a storied American shipbuilding tradition that produced some of the fastest and most beautiful ships in history. It included the famous *America*, which in 1851, won the cup that would bear its name in yacht racing history to the present day. *America*, almost exactly *Halcyon*'s size, carried about the same amount of sail area on its two schooner-rigged masts. Had Captain Hall used the celebrated *America* as a model for his *Halcyon* or just been inspired by it, as were other builders of the time? There's no way of knowing, but the similarities are obvious, and the result, a very, very fast sailing vessel perhaps the fastest ever built on the West Coast—are identical.

By May 1883, *Halcyon* was ready and beautifully finished, a yacht fit for a millionaire and more, an oceangoing, blue-water speed machine. Spectators years later would gaze at the schooner after it arrived home after a transoceanic voyage and marvel that it looked as if it had just come from a turn around the harbor. That is a tribute to Winslow Hall and William Stone, who knew how to build boats.

While Stone worked, owner Tevis made some staffing arrangements, and he wasn't taking any chances on losing those upcoming match races with the other gentlemen of the Pacific Yacht Club. Tevis started with a captain, and he found a good one in George Cummings. A true master mariner, Cummings had been on the ocean for thirty years, most recently in command of the famous clipper ship *Three Brothers*, reputedly the largest sailing vessel in the world. Cummings was comfortable enough in the smaller schooner and found a crew to help him work Tevis's little ship, and by the end of April, everything was ready for *Halcyon*'s debut.

William I. Stone shipyard, Hunter's Point. *California State Library.*

On Friday, May 4, *Halcyon* hit the waters of San Francisco Bay, sliding down the ways at Stone's Shipyard at Hunter's Point as Tevis held a celebratory party, champagne and hors d'oeuvres marking the occasion. The schooner wasn't ready to sail immediately—there are always little details that must be addressed once the ship is in the water—but it must have been very satisfying to see this beautiful creation finally in its natural element.

Halcyon went outside the Heads its first week on the water, but before that, it won its first race with stiff new sails, taut lines, tight pulleys and a crew just feeling its way through the motions needed to make this racing machine work. Tevis quickly learned the price of its speed, for there was a price. *Halcyon* was wet, though Hall and Stone and Cummings would have already known this. With no deckhouse, the only yacht on the bay of that design, the smooth deck passed any water that came over the rails from side to side and front to back, wetting everything—and everyone—in the way. In the gate, a green sea climbed aboard, a taste of what waited offshore. Dry in the cockpit, Cummings ignored the water and looked aloft, wondering if it'd take more sail if he could get another knot or two out of it. And builder Stone was pleased. His little ship was shaking off these waves, the water sluicing away as planned, the deck carefully caulked and not letting a drop into the luxurious spaces below.

Owner Harry Tevis was not so charmed. Perhaps he was imagining the faces of his younger female guests, seeing their shock and hearing the shrieks as *Halcyon* buried its bow in a long, gray swell and a ton of white water came foaming aft. In the bay, where the winds can be fierce but the waves don't have enough room to pile higher than a couple of feet, *Halcyon* would shine. Here, it would be at home as a yacht, a sporting man's pleasure craft, rounding the racing marks in dignity and style, miles ahead of its nearest competitors, only some spray flying across her decks. Outside, past the Farallon Islands, it would sail like a witch, yes, but all in the ship would pay a price.

Within days, there would be challenges, races to Monterey and around the Farallon Islands and back home to the bay. The gentlemen of the Pacific Club (especially those who wouldn't be going) wanted a real trial—Tevis and *Halcyon* against the Spreckels' new *Lurline* on a match race all the way to Hawaii. It would have been a fine test, and he might have set a record to last one hundred years, but Harry Tevis had neither the time nor the inclination to take his little ship so far from home. He made the short trips to Monterey and Santa Cruz, up and down the bay, and a year later, Tevis had enough. On June 13, 1884, the San Francisco papers reported that he sold *Halcyon* to Joseph Grant and Robert F. Morrow for $10,000.

Joseph Grant was a dry goods merchant, son of a California pioneer who had sold clothing to Gold Rush San Francisco and whose sons now held forth from Murphy, Grant & Company, a major dry goods wholesaler supplying other businesses throughout California and as far north as Alaska.

Robert F. Morrow bought an interest in *Halcyon* for his sons. Morrow, fifty-nine that year and a little old to begin playing with boats himself, had three boys at home, the oldest eighteen. Their mother had died five years earlier, and Morrow, a stockbroker and principal in the Sutter Street Railroad, had extensive business interests in the city and ranch property in Santa Clara. Neither of the new owners was really a seaman, and this was the 1884 equivalent of giving a Ferrari to a pair of Sunday school teachers. Predictably, *Halcyon* took on a new placid role, one that mostly stayed away from the perils of the open ocean.

The *Daily Alta California* newspaper summed up its new story well in its personals column a few months later, on April 13, 1885. The headline alone, "Miss Crocker's Yachting Party," was enough to make any real sailor-man weep. It read, "A delightful sail around the bay was enjoyed last Saturday by a small party of the younger members of society, who, at the invitation of Miss Hattie Crocker, were passengers on the 11:30 o'clock boat for Saucelito, where the natty yacht known as the *Halcyon* awaited them. Joseph D. Grant, the owner of the craft, kindly placed it at the disposal of Miss Crocker for entertainment purposes."

The schooner's days as a party barge continued through 1886, and on May 24, the newspapers reported, "Joseph D. Grant entertained a party of friends on his yacht *Halcyon*, one day last week. A delightful breakfast on the yacht and a sail around the bay were among the pleasures of the day." One can imagine the scene, a gathering of beautifully attired guests tended to by liveried servants, *Halcyon*'s professional crew waiting to take the group on a sedate turn around Alcatraz and back to the pier. It's the portrait of a life of wealth and leisure, but other distractions threatened this pleasant picture.

Morrow had some major legal problems, starting with labor trouble on his Sutter Street Railroad—one of San Francisco's famed cable car routes. In one incident, a dynamite blast paralyzed a woman, and in another, someone gunned down an innocent bystander at a picket line. The police department suspected that the shooting had started on Morrow's orders, and they charged his superintendent with manslaughter.

Trouble inched closer to Morrow himself when a man fell through a hole at the rail yard, breaking his neck. The widow sued, and Morrow threw in the towel with surprising and somewhat suspicious ease. Suspicion turned to outrage when the jury awarded the widow a paltry $7,500, the newspapers hinting the whole thing had been rigged from the beginning. A few days later, Morrow and several employees were indicted for fixing the jury in a criminal case that would drag on throughout 1887. He eventually won an acquittal, but having his passengers blown up and his superintendents jailed limited Morrow's time for gadding about on the bay. By the end of 1886, he wanted to unload his schooner yacht.

This time, there were no takers among the other wealthy yachtsmen of San Francisco. On March 31, 1887, the *Sausalito News* passed the sad word to its readers in the yachting community: "The fleet has been materially weakened by the sale of the schooner *Halcyon*." San Francisco's fastest yacht would no longer grace the clubs and the regattas on the bay.

Its new owners applied to the Treasury Department to place *Halcyon* on the Register of Merchant Vessels of the United States. Builder Stone filled out a carpenter's certificate describing the ship he'd created in 1883, though, curiously, all of the official documents showed 1887 as the build year. It was almost as if the schooner had been born again. Perhaps it had, as the paperwork came back assigning *Halcyon* register number 95914, which it would carry to its grave, and listing its new owner as a shadowy, almost anonymous individual named Albert W. Wilson. Although it wasn't obvious at the time (which was exactly how he and his friends wanted it), Wilson was the front man for some others even more mysterious. He quickly turned the schooner over to its new master.

It took the skipper a few months to fit the vessel out for its new role. No more yachting parties and breakfast turns about the bay. No more leisurely cruises down the coast to Santa Cruz or Monterey—just hard work and careful preparation, and when these were finally finished, it was time to sail. On August 10, 1887, *Halcyon* slipped away from its mooring and out into the Golden Gate.

2

MASTER MARINER

A LIFE ON THE ROCKS

The hand of a master mariner gripped the helm that August morning as *Halcyon* burst between the Heads, turning north, not for the "hunting and fishing" waters that it had declared on its papers but toward Victoria, British Columbia, 750 nautical miles distant. Alfred Metcalf had been at sea, or at least on the water, for the better part of thirty years, making him a key man—maybe *the* key man at this point—in the opium ring. After all, in 1887, anyone could walk into any of a dozen perfectly legal businesses on Cormorant or Government Streets in Victoria and buy as much opium as he or she could afford. And the same person could go to Chinatown in San Francisco and sell that same opium at a neat and perfectly legal profit all day long. But unless you planned to pay the duty—and the men of the opium ring did not—all that opium wasn't going anywhere without *Halcyon*, and *Halcyon* wasn't going anywhere without Captain Alfred B. Metcalf.

Metcalf turned fifty-five that year, not changing careers, exactly, but definitely changing his life. Up to a point, that life had followed the steady and predictable course that every ship's captain likes to see, but lately, there had been more than a few rocks and shoals. He was born in Chardon, Ohio, a farm boy a long way from the ocean, into a family of eleven children but left home for the sea. He did his apprentice work on the East Coast, sailing out of New York, where he met Katharina, a Prussian woman who was already a widow with two daughters, before he moved to San Francisco, setting up on the West Coast right before the Civil War. He established himself quickly and then brought his young family west to California for opportunities in

San Francisco's booming maritime trade. Like many mariners, he'd worked his way up from seaman to ship's officer, and in San Francisco, he'd been made first mate on the ninety-eight-ton steamer SS *Salinas* in 1864.

This was a very promising position. Not only did it hold out the prospect of an eventual promotion to master—every ship's officer's goal—but *Salinas* was also part of a small and growing fleet owned by Goodall and Nelson, a little outfit with big plans. The company started out servicing ships in the San Francisco Bay area, providing freshwater from Sausalito and then entering the coasting trade with *Salinas*, its first steamer. It made regular trips out through the Golden Gate and down to Monterey, with stops in between, for the next twenty years, carrying freight and a few passengers and adding ships as it went.

Metcalf did get his promotion; by 1867, he was captain of *Salinas*, a position he would hold for seven years, and he was still with the company when it expanded again in 1874, taking on a partner and becoming the Goodall, Nelson & Perkins Steamship Company (GN&P). It immediately bought six large steamships from its rival, the Pacific Mail Steamship Company, and picked up some smaller ones, too, which gave GN&P new reach away from the Bay Area and the near California coast all the way to Washington, British Columbia and Alaska and as far south as San Diego. A year later, reorganizing as the Pacific Coast Steamship Company, it served twenty ports in California alone. Life must have looked very promising for Captain Metcalf, now sailing as master of the steam schooner *Gipsy* and making regular runs to ports up and down the coast.

Gipsy, though bigger, at 239 tons, and sturdier than *Salinas*, was hardly the pride of the line, which had bigger, more luxurious ships on more prestigious routes, but it provided the captain with valuable experience, eventually earning him some recognition as "one of the best schooner sailors on the Coast." *Gipsy* plied the Pacific waters as far north as Washington and on its regular run down the coast to San Diego, stopping at ports along the way. At *Gipsy*'s wheel, Metcalf learned every harbor, anchorage and cove, every haven and hazard to navigators from Oregon to Mexico.

Every year, called to list his name, address and occupation, Metcalf did so, proudly describing himself as "sea captain" or "master mariner," and throughout the 1860s and 1870s, both claims were accurate. In 1875, though, the sea got a lot farther away for Captain Metcalf. There's no official report, no newspaper account of a grounding or a collision, some trivial or terrible mistake that cost the passengers their lives and the captain his ship and his career, but on March 5, 1875, *Gipsy* went into drydock for repairs, and when it sailed again on March 16, a new skipper had the helm. Metcalf's command and that promising future with Goodall, Nelson disappeared.

There was a hint of the troubles, as newspapers commented on the captain's hobby, describing him as "rather under-sized, wiry, cool and close-mouthed.…He could hold his own on the drink but liquor never loosened his tongue or made his head flighty." Another story said, "He could stow away sixteen glasses of grog below his hatchways without winking an eyelid."

The drinking cost him more than his job; he lost his wife and family too. By 1879, Metcalf had moved to a cheap boardinghouse for sailors and workingmen near the waterfront. Soon after, Katharina, still in the fine house on Silver Street, was going by "Catherine" and listing herself in the city directory as a widow, a claim she would steadfastly maintain for the rest of her life.

There were jobs for fallen sea captains, even drunks, and one turned up. Metcalf signed on as master of the harbor tugboat *Favorite*. It was one of the older tugs on the bay, barely big enough to allow Metcalf to make his

Tugboat *Favorite*. Alfred Metcalf, master, at San Francisco, February 1879. *Drawing by Carlos J. Hittell, University of California, Berkeley.*

usual "sea captain" claim in that year's directory. But the job didn't last, and he moved to the *Richard Holyoke*, another tugboat, and finally to the *Joseph H. Redmond*, an old steam tug that had been on the bay almost as long as Metcalf himself.

He stayed with the *Redmond* the longest, four years at the wheel, servicing the bigger ships he'd once taken to and from the sea from these same docks, but on August 10, 1887, Alfred Metcalf had a chance to turn the world back up again as he sailed *Halcyon* out through the Golden Gate.

He began outfitting *Halcyon* back in Sausalito, starting with the sailing rig, replacing the sails with heavier canvas and strengthened rigging, preparing the ship for the clandestine trips it would be making in the rough seas and higher winds between British Columbia and San Francisco. By August, Metcalf had done everything a master mariner knew had to be done to turn a pleasure yacht into something more and now he and his partners looked ahead.

In *Halcyon*, he would take his ship, its crew and its contraband cargo on long, tedious passages followed by the dangerous dance of an unpowered sailing vessel off an unforgiving coastline with only the moon and the stars for light. He had to navigate precisely to get *Halcyon* to the right place in an empty ocean at the appointed time to meet another dark ship in the night. He had to make sure that everything worked exactly as planned; they'd be landing cargo and people in small boats ashore through surf, an undertaking so hazardous that it would kill at least one crewman. And he had to prepare to deal with any revenue cutters on patrol and customs men on the lookout for smugglers.

There was plenty that could go wrong, mistakes that might cost everyone's freedom or maybe their lives and the always looming threat of death at sea, but on that bright morning in August, Metcalf rested his hand on the wheel and felt his little ship slicing cleanly through the Pacific swells past the Seal Rocks and out through the Golden Gate. With *Halcyon* at sea at last, the opium ring was in business.

3

WHOLESALE DRUGGIST IN THE AGE OF DRUGS

As Metcalf sailed away from San Francisco, the ring's second key man made arrangements to sell the cargo *Halcyon* had gone to collect. Born in Japan in September 1863, Ewen Wainwright McLean's father was superintendent of the lighthouse service in Nagasaki, and the family—at the time just father Hugh, mother Sarah, sister Ellen and baby Ewen—lived in the small, tight foreign community that was established in 1855.

Westerners with families found conditions in Japan far from ideal for children, who were expected to grow up in their own culture and not one as foreign as Japan's. Nagasaki provided little opportunity for the education of young White children, so when Ewen was old enough, around age five, his family sent him off to what would then have been one of the nearest schools, St. Paul's College in Hong Kong.

St. Paul's, an Anglican school for boys founded in 1851, still graduates students today. In the late 1860s and early 1870s, the school taught English and other subjects to Chinese boys, as well as taking White students like Ewen. In 1873, St. Paul's changed its mission to focus mainly on English-speaking boys, as Hong Kong's White population grew in that period, but by that time, Ewen had already benefited from years with the Chinese students. He had become fluent in Cantonese, learning it at almost the same age that Chinese boys do and communicating daily with people from the part of China that sent the majority of emigrants to the United States, Hawaii and Canada. Most of these people learned and spoke the same dialect and used the same idioms, expressions and slang. McLean's Hong Kong education became an extremely useful asset in at least two of his future careers.

McLean did not get the chance to graduate with his class at St. Paul's, however, as his father died in 1875. Ewen's mother moved with the other children, now three of them, to San Francisco, and Ewen followed in 1876. By 1880, the entire family was living together on Dupont Street at the edge of Chinatown.

Hugh McLean's death left the family in straitened conditions, which meant that young Ewen needed to go to work as soon as he could to help support his mother. He found a job at sixteen, starting his business career as a clerk with Crane & Brigham, wholesale druggists. The stock in trade for both Crane & Brigham and Redington Company, the two original drug companies in San Francisco, took the form of patent and proprietary medicines. America had a real drug and addiction problem in the 1880s, and these medicines and the opium in them lay at the very heart of it.

This was the heyday of the snake oil salesman, the quack, the phony panacea, the cure-all that cured nothing, what reformer Samuel Hopkins Adams a few years later called the "Great American Fraud." Medicine itself was transforming, the occupations of physician, surgeon and pharmacist becoming true professions with real standards, training and regulation in the last decades of the nineteenth century, while advances in biology, chemistry and pharmacy promised new and more effective treatments for conditions that had plagued mankind for thousands of years.

Professionally trained and educated physicians in the new century would soon have tools that could effect unprecedented, even miraculous cures, but in 1880, almost the only remedy that actually worked reliably was the same one that had for three thousand years—opium. The drug gave those in pain immediate relief, and doctors could treat coughs and diarrhea, too, both still major health issues—and killers—in the 1800s. Opium didn't actually cure any of the conditions that created these symptoms, though one would never know this from the advertisements and wild claims of the drug manufacturers, but because opium worked and almost nothing else did, it was the default ingredient in thousands of nostrums sold all across America.

These drugs were widely available, not just from older and established companies like Redington or Crane & Brigham but also from small pharmacies, grocery stores and other places where patent and proprietary medicines were sold, which in 1887, was just about everywhere. People

Collier's

THE NATIONAL WEEKLY

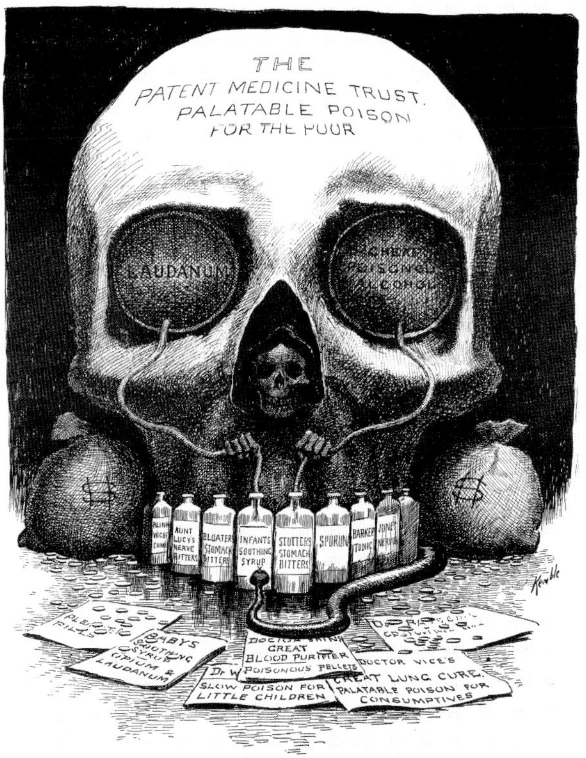

DEATH'S LABORATORY

Patent medicines are poisoning people throughout America to-day. Babies who cry are fed laudanum under the name of syrup. Women are led to injure themselves for life by reading in the papers about the meaning of backache. Young men and boys are robbed and contaminated by vicious criminals who lure them to their dens through seductive advertisements

DRAWN BY E. W. KEMBLE

Collier's magazine series on patent medicines in 1905 led to passage of the Pure Food and Drug Act. *Author's collection.*

could even order them by mail. Almost no government restrictions impeded the traffic, and as a young clerk at Crane & Brigham and later at Redington, McLean undoubtedly sold bottles containing alcohol, opium, morphine and cocaine without a prescription to anyone—man, woman or child—who wanted them every day of the week.

Many of these people were addicts; no one really knows how many, hundreds of thousands at least, perhaps a million or more. In 1887, America imported 568,263 pounds—284 tons—of opium, an almost 400,000-pound increase in only fifteen years. Drug companies compounded most of it into medicines such as laudanum, an ancient and effective combination of alcohol and opium, although some was further refined into morphine that companies sold over the counter or by mail with hypodermic syringes.

McLean branched out in 1885, purchasing all of the stock and equipment of the Davis Manufacturing Company, a maker of proprietary medicines, going into business as E.W. McLean & Co. A year later, he partnered with William H. Cork, an English druggist, forming W.H. Cork & Co., Druggists and Apothecaries, marketing a medication for corns called a Warren's London Corn Cure. McLean, however, used his new company to go into an entirely separate area of the drug business. He was in the addiction department.

America had two types of drug addicts in the 1880s, and at W.H Cork & Co., McLean proposed to address both of them. The first group were those Americans hooked by overuse of patent, proprietary or other medicines containing opium or morphine. The second, and much narrower addiction subset, was found among those who used drugs for what we today call "recreational" purposes, essentially the taking of narcotics with the intent of "getting high." In 1887, the choices for this option were fairly limited. Some people did abuse morphine, cocaine and chloral hydrate, but for the most part, recreational drug users in the period smoked opium, and almost all of the drug users were Chinese.

Although the newspapers eagerly reported on any White people who happened to be caught in the dens, this occurred relatively infrequently. In Hawaii, arrest statistics showed that Chinese smokers and den-keepers accounted for over 90 percent of the opium-related offenses, and in some years, the number was as high as 96 percent.

Some White people did frequent the dens and became the "opium fiends" that the newspaper reporters loved to spotlight. When San Francisco passed its ordinance banning the keeping or frequenting of opium dens on November 30, 1875, the first such law in the United States, it didn't take long for the police to round up some violators. At 2:00 a.m. on December 6 at 609 Dupont Street, Fannie Whitmore, Cora Martinez, James Dennison, Charles Anderson and "two Chinamen keeping the place" had the dubious distinction of becoming America's very first arrestees in its now 130-plus-year war on drugs. Millions would follow, but with what can only be regarded at this point as charming innocence, the newspaperman on the scene that

San Francisco Police Chinatown squad, 1898. *Bancroft Library, University of California, Berkeley.*

long-ago morning optimistically reported that the "police intend to continue their raids until the growing evil is suppressed."

For Ewen McLean, both the medical and the recreational markets for opium represented big opportunities. In 1887, Hawaii imported at least five tons of smoking opium to support a Chinese population of twenty-one thousand. In the United States, thirty-three tons entered through customs, almost all of it at the port of San Francisco. Actual demand was even higher, and quite a bit more was being smuggled, and McLean went looking for sources to supply this demand.

Smoking opium in this period came almost exclusively from poppy fields and the opium monopoly of British India. The crude or raw opium was gathered from the fields of India's Malwa and Patna regions and then shipped by sea to Hong Kong, Canton or other Chinese ports, where it would be further refined into either the smoking or medicinal form. Once at Hong Kong and nearby Portuguese Macao, the opium traveled by ship to Chinese communities in the Straits Settlements, Australia, Tahiti, Panama, Canada, Cuba, Hawaii and to the Gold Mountains of California.

The monopolies in Hong Kong and Macao usually boxed opium in small rectangular cans or tins, sealed with solder or wax, each one containing five *taels* or 6.66 ounces of opium. Each "half-pound tin" assessed a five-dollar duty (ten dollars per pound in 1885). The 1885 gold standard for prepared opium was a Hong Kong brand called Lai Yuen, shipped by the local monopoly to ports around the Pacific. Lai Yuen tins were stamped with a distinctive mark on the lid, and the cans each had a paper label in Chinese that advertised the brand. These tins fetched premium prices in the Hawaii and San Francisco markets, but sellers didn't have to go all the way to Hong Kong to get Lai Yuen opium, although it was considerably cheaper in the crown colony. At least nine opium dealers operated openly in Victoria, British Columbia, with more in Nanaimo, Westminster and Vancouver. Some imported Lai Yuen and others that prepared their own high-quality opium from the crude, one manufacturer refining opium daily just two doors down from the city hall and police department.

Another option was Hawaii, where the law banned importation, sale and possession, except for medicinal use on a doctor's prescription. Prohibition drove Hawaii's opium traffic underground and raised prices, a situation familiar to Americans today. Smugglers took advantage of the much higher black-market prices in the islands by shipping prepared opium concealed in commercial cargoes from Hong Kong, Canada and even San Francisco, getting most of it past the poorly funded, inefficient and corrupt Hawaiian customs service.

On June 30, 1885, officers in Honolulu got lucky and seized 3,200 tins concealed in packages of "cuttlefish and lily flour" aboard the bark *Centaur*, just arrived from Hong Kong. The shipment had been consigned to Honolulu businessman and importer Leong Pang. He promptly pleaded guilty, receiving a $400 fine and nine months at hard labor, which left the opium resting in government custody in Honolulu. In a well-intentioned effort to earn the kingdom a little money by selling it abroad, the government held an auction.

Ewen McLean paid $4,000, for almost a ton of good quality smoking opium, far less, at a little more than $2 per pound, than the going rate of $6 to $7 per pound in Victoria and $12 to $15 in San Francisco. He didn't plan on paying any American customs duties on his shipment, either, which he saw safely aboard the SS *Mariposa* on November 14. McLean marked his crates with "In Transit for Panama," creating paperwork consigning the shipment to the SS *Colima*, a steamer that made a regular run to the Isthmus from San Francisco.

It's possible that McLean really intended for his ton of opium to go to Panama, where hundreds of Chinese laborers were busy digging and dying on Ferdinand de Lesseps's ill-fated canal project. It's far more likely, almost certain in fact, that he planned to have someone sneak his shipment off the *Mariposa* or out of the bonded warehouse while it sat, supposedly waiting for the *Colima* to arrive and collect it for its next leg to Panama. For that,

McLean needed insider access to the warehouse or the ship, and he had such access. Some of his closest associates worked for the United States Customs Service at the Custom House in San Francisco. And so did Ewen McLean.

He first went to work for customs as a part-time Chinese translator in January 1884, even before he became a naturalized U.S. citizen in June of that year. At the time, customs handled immigration matters, and in San Francisco, this meant dealing with Chinese people. McLean's ability to speak fluent Cantonese was a huge asset; not many White people in California had any grasp of the language, and although both customs and the San Francisco Police used Chinese translators in their enforcement activities, they never completely trusted them.

McLean worked in the registration division, and he fell right in with a group of corrupt inspectors that included William "Champagne Billy" Boyd and Ferdinand Ciprico, but his closest associate and future business partner was an assistant to the port's surveyor, Will Whaley.

By November, when the *Mariposa* arrived from Honolulu with McLean's opium aboard, collector John Hager had uncovered a scandal in his port, one involving immigration fraud. Hager thought the corruption reached at least as far as his part-time translator, whom he promptly fired, and when McLean's ship came in on November 22, customs didn't take any chances with those crates marked "In Transit for Panama." Collector Hager ordered the seizure of the entire shipment for nonpayment of the ten-dollars-per-pound duty.

McLean hired a lawyer and sued, arguing that goods in transit *from* a foreign country *to* a foreign country were not subject to duty. Although the lawsuit took two years to wind its way through federal district and appeals courts, the judges ruled in McLean's favor, eventually awarding him $3,700 in 1887 for his losses. In 1890, Congress finally appropriated taxpayer money to pay Ewen McLean back for the opium he'd intended to smuggle, and by that time, McLean was a full-time opium smuggler, defrauding the United States Treasury of many times that amount.

McLean's first venture into Hawaiian waters had ended rather badly, with a ton of his opium seized by the customs division, but it marked a significant moment for the opium ring that he and Will Whaley began to construct. The venture put Chinese-speaking McLean in contact with the Chinese traders and public officials in Honolulu and gave him a close look at how the black market for opium functioned in the kingdom. As the New Year approached, the now-unemployed former customs officers, though under investigation for official corruption, moved full time into the opium business, chasing easy money from a familiar source.

4

"MY GOD, I'M SHOT!"

THE RUBBER MAN

Shortly after 1:00 a.m. on October 24, 1882, a Whitehall rowing boat slipped with muffled oars through the dark waters under the Pacific Mail Steamship pier at the foot of Folsom Street in San Francisco. The two men aboard the Whitehall showed no lights and made no sound as they eased up alongside the steamship *Arabic*, in port three days on its latest voyage from Asia. Customs surveyor John Morton, well aware that ships like *Arabic* on the Hong Kong run invariably brought opium and other undeclared valuables somewhere on board, routinely stationed inspectors aboard the ship and on the piers nearby for the duration of their stays in San Francisco.

On this morning, six inspectors, almost the entire night watch, reported for duty at midnight at *Arabic*'s berth. Edward McLean, an experienced officer, had a roving patrol that covered the ship and the Pacific Mail dock. John Dawes was posted on the pier at the foot of the freight plank. James Rourke had a position on the dock covering the side of the steamer facing the pier while John Babcock had the main deck of the 430-foot ship. Night inspector C.A. Harper patrolled a lower deck while another officer, Hinshaw, rowed the customhouse Whitehall in the black waters nearby.

None of them knew that the dreaded Rubber Man was also aboard the *Arabic* that night, and none raised any alarm as the rowboat eased out from under the pier into the overhang of *Arabic*'s bow to a line hanging down to the water. The two men in the Whitehall shipped their oars as someone aboard the steamer began passing packages through a darkened porthole down to the waiting boat.

SS *Arabic*, built in 1881, was a new ship when Will Whaley made his October 1882 arrest and seizure. The White Star liner was later sold and sailed as SS *Saarndam*. *Author's collection.*

Rourke should have seen the boat's approach; he was only yards away from the action and just above the hanging line, but he was silent until he suddenly saw movement on top of one of the deck structures.

"Say, say, there's a man on the whaleback," he called, alerting the rest of the watch not to the smugglers in the boat but to a danger closer at hand.

The Rubber Man jumped to the deck and ran to the side of the ship, ordering the men in the boat to halt. "Stop where you are or I'll shoot," he shouted down, but the two boatmen laid to their oars and pulled away as William Whaley pulled the trigger. The first cartridge in the revolver misfired, but shots rang out with the second and third.

"My God, I'm shot!" cried one of the smugglers as he dropped his oars.

His partner pulled harder. Edward McLean joined Whaley at the ship's rail, the two inspectors watching as the boat vanished into the darkness.

When the customhouse boat arrived, Hinshaw had little to do but retrieve the packages thrown overboard during the escape. This proved to be quite a haul—300 pounds of prepared opium, 123 pounds of unrefined opium, 500 silk handkerchiefs and silk cord, all valued at over $6,000. The two smugglers—one wounded—managed to escape, but their confederate aboard the *Arabic* wasn't so lucky. Whaley pointed out that James Rourke had been stationed only feet from the hanging line, and he had called the warning to the men below. Hearing Whaley's account later that morning, surveyor Morton fired Rourke and ordered his arrest. The *Arabic* case would be just the latest in a line of triumphs for Will Whaley, the hardworking and conscientious inspector that customs officers and smugglers alike called the Rubber Man.

William Alexander Whaley was born at Arcata, California, on April 18, 1861, the youngest of three children. His father, John A. Whaley, a butcher by trade, went to Arcata—then known as Union—with the earliest settlers, chasing the gold bug when it led them into the Klamath, Trinity and Salmon mountains to the east of town. On Humboldt Bay, the port serviced first the gold mines and later the logging industry in the area.

John Whaley had bigger plans for himself and his family and began by leaving the meat business and his harness and saddlery sideline and going into the civil service, initially as Union's postmaster. He also served as a notary public, justice of the peace and town recorder, but in 1864, he received the plum appointment as a deputy collector of the United States Bureau of Internal Revenue, a position he would hold for twenty-five years.

Whaley's district covered Trinity, Humboldt and Del Norte Counties and took him as far north as the Oregon border. Like virtually all federal jobs at the time, his was a political patronage position, and Whaley was a staunch Republican, active in party politics and member of California's Republican State Central Committee. These political connections and the position with Internal Revenue would be useful when his son went looking for a job at the Treasury Department fifteen years later.

Son Will joined daughters Emma, born in 1856, and Martha Jane, born two years later. The girls' mother, Emily, kept the family's house, a neat, two-story Greek revival–style home, designed and built by John Whaley in 1855 on a plateau just a few blocks north of Union's central plaza.

Will Whaley got the nickname "Wash" early in life, growing up in the bustling lumber town that flourished as the trade in redwood grew throughout the 1860s and 1870s. To accommodate both steamships and the lumber schooners that carried logs away from the town, Arcata built a long wharf out into the deep water of Humboldt Bay. The town boasted California's first railroad, a horse-drawn affair with tracks from the plaza to the wharf, and it had a school, Arcata Union High, which all three Whaley children attended.

Big sister Martha didn't graduate but married at sixteen and moved with Patrick McGowan, an older, worldly New York journalist, to San Francisco in 1874, when Will was thirteen. She had two sons in short order, but she died young, and their overwhelmed father sent the boys back to grow up in their

Arcata, California, looking northwest from the Plaza toward the Whaley house. *Humboldt State University Library.*

mother's home in Arcata. Oldest sister Emma never married, staying in the family home with her parents and helping to raise Martha's boys until 1883, when a fall from her horse killed her. These family trials would become both relevant and very publicly poignant after John Whaley died in 1888, leaving mother Emily struggling alone to raise the two grandsons while her only son abandoned the family to become rich in the dope business.

Will grew to a shade under six feet, "powerfully built" and developing the boisterous, oversized personality that reporters and others would remark on over the years. He made friends easily in Arcata, notably Louis Greenwald, who lived a block away and was two classes behind Will in school. Both boys moved away from their small town after graduation for the brighter lights and better opportunities in the big city.

San Francisco, with its population of almost a quarter million, was booming in 1879, when eighteen-year-old Wash Whaley arrived. With the transcontinental railroad completed, reliable steamship service throughout the Pacific and rail links up and down the West Coast, the promise of California, America's Golden State, was only just beginning to be realized. Jobs were plentiful, especially for a young man from a good family with connections. Will took a room at the Brooklyn Hotel on Bush Street and enrolled in the nearby Heald's Business College. After only two months, he found work as a bookkeeper, though this job wouldn't last, as he pursued his real ambition, gaining employment with the federal government.

Positions at the Treasury Department and other government agencies were not subject to modern civil service rules at the time, and presidential appointees, like San Francisco collector Eugene L. Sullivan, routinely made hiring decisions based on political and social connections. Whaley's father, a Treasury employee and relatively prominent in state Republican Party politics, would ordinarily have had some influence with Sullivan, but things were more complicated in 1880, as times were changing in federal service.

Republican Rutherford B. Hayes became the nineteenth president of the United States in 1876, carrying California. His election normally would have secured the positions of Republican appointees like John Whaley, but the new president started his term with a promise to reform what he saw as a corrupt and mismanaged federal civil service system. John Whaley's job would be safe—he continued on as a deputy collector of Internal Revenue until his death in 1888—but landing his son a job in the Treasury Department was more problematic because President Hayes kicked off his reform campaign by taking aim at the notoriously crooked and inefficient Treasury Division of Customs.

Hayes's first target was the New York Custom House, the most corrupt in the entire country and packed to the rafters with political cronies, shiftless do-nothings and out-and-out crooks. In fact, at least one person remarked that the only honest employee (out of more than four hundred) in the New York Custom House was an inspector named Herman Melville who whiled away idle hours writing an epic poem to follow his novel *Moby Dick* instead of hunting up opportunities for graft like everyone else.

Hayes began by trying to fire the top three people in the Custom House, who all defied him and refused to leave. (This included collector Chester A. Arthur, who went on to become the twenty-first president of the United States.) Hayes appointed replacements. The Senate refused to confirm them. The frustrated president found that at least 20 percent of the employees in New York were superfluous political cronies of the state's powerful senator Roscoe Conkling, but Hayes couldn't get rid of them, either. It took two years, but he gradually weeded out the top ranks of the Customs Service and replaced the old political appointees with his own (presumably better) political appointees.

In San Francisco, collector Sullivan had been appointed in 1880 to oversee the largest port on the West Coast and its over two hundred employees. Sullivan, a New York attorney, delegated hiring decisions, especially those for the position of night inspector, among the lowliest in the service, to his surveyor, John M. Morton. The surveyor, who would become Whaley's mentor in the service, certainly understood politics and patronage. The son of an Indiana governor and senator, Morton had been a special agent for the Treasury Department in Alaska before moving to customs in San Francisco, where he ran the inspection force at the port.

When it came to his latest applicant, Morton got some input from the deputy collector of internal revenue up in Arcata and from Patrick McGowan, a local newspaper editor and Will Whaley's brother-in-law. With at least two people leaning on him, Morton hired the strapping young man as a night inspector. It was the first step on the government ladder.

Will Whaley's initial assignment was definitely one of those bottom-of-the-ladder-rungs. Back in the time of steam and sail, a squad of regular customs inspectors met ships coming into the bay from abroad at a quarantine point in the bay. In San Francisco, this was at Meiggs Wharf at the foot of Powell Street. They searched anyone leaving the ship, passengers and crew, along with their baggage, and any cargo being discharged. The inspectors also gave the ship itself a good going-over, looking in all the nooks and crannies in a process that might take a day or even several, depending on the ship's size and the number of passengers or the cargo. But there was no hurry;

Woman showing baggage contents to Customs officer, New York 1909. *Library of Congress.*

unlike modern airplanes, the ship wasn't turning around and going right back out in a few hours. Instead, it might linger in port for several days if it was a Pacific Mail or other steamship on a regularly scheduled route or even a couple of weeks or months if it was tramp, waiting for repairs or for a cargo or a crew.

The night inspectors focused on these ships anchored offshore or tied up at one of San Francisco's dozens of piers or wharves. There, an inspector might be stationed aboard the vessel or assigned to one of the piers. Commanded by a captain, the night shift had two watches of about eight men each, supervised by a lieutenant. A commenter from the time said: "The duties of night inspectors as defined by the regulations appear to be essentially those of watchmen. They are appointed to prevent smuggling and to watch over vessels, stores or merchandise in their custody—to prevent the landing of any merchandise from any vessel between sunset and sunrise, unless the same is done by proper authority and under a day inspector's supervision."

It could be an awfully boring job, and it didn't pay much. By federal law, the inspectors got "three dollars for each night's service." They wore a distinctive uniform on duty, one for the summer and one for winter, and the cost, fifty dollars, came out of the new night inspector's pocket.

The night man did have a financial incentive to be vigilant. Like the regular inspectors, he could receive 25 percent of the proceeds of the sale of any merchandise he seized. This included smoking opium. The increase of the duty on opium in 1883 boosted smuggling dramatically, but even before that, there were still plenty of passengers and crewmen trying to sneak a few (or a few thousand) five-tael tins through the port. People tried to slip cigars and silk, lace, brandy, gloves, diamonds and assorted other items past the officers, too, but in San Francisco, the steady reward money for the inspectors was in opium.

Whaley spent a year learning the ropes. He and his colleagues reported one day at around sunset and worked until midnight, and the following night reporting at 11:00 p.m. and worked until dawn. These alternating "short and long days off" were supposed to make up for the seven-day work week.

To keep the inspectors from getting too cozy with the ships' crews or the workers on the piers, the lieutenants moved them around, seldom posting the night men to the same ship or wharf for two shifts running. The lieutenants had to be on the lookout for other problems. It was well known that many of the men found warm places to curl up and sleep for most of their shifts, and others regularly abandoned their posts for the comfort of the saloons that lined the streets just behind the wharves.

The Pacific Mail Steamship wharf, San Francisco, site of the notorious opium seizure from the SS *City of Tokio*. *Bancroft Library, University of California, Berkeley.*

Whaley made at least one friend in Ferdinand Ciprico, another night inspector, and more importantly, he hadn't gotten tangled up with the nine officers whose negligence or venality cost them their jobs in March 1882. As usual, in San Francisco, it started with opium, a big haul—Edward Egan's 3,880 five-tael tin catch from the SS *City of Tokio*. Normally, the seizure of almost two tons of prime smoking opium would be cause for considerable celebration in the Custom House, but Egan didn't work for customs; he and his partners were San Francisco police officers who had been on harbor patrol the night they came across some suspicious characters in a small boat.

This prompted some uncomfortable questions from the newspapers. Had the customs men been bribed to look the other way or were they simply too incompetent to notice almost a ton of opium as it floated around the harbor? None of the answers made collector Sullivan, surveyor Morton or their men look very good, and an embarrassed Treasury Department detailed a special agent to get to the bottom of the whole mess. Even before he had any answers, Morton shook up the night force, firing the captain and the lieutenant and six of the eight inspectors who had been on duty the night of the *City of Tokio* seizure. Will Whaley, one of the two survivors, rode out the scandal unscathed.

With Morton's support, Will set out to impress his superiors with his diligence. Six months later, on September 4, 1882, just after 2:00 a.m., he and a couple other night inspectors took another look at the SS *Coptic*, a Pacific Mail steamer that had been checked several times before. This time, Whaley hit the jackpot, finding 3,955 silk handkerchiefs, eighty-three silk sashes, a package of clothing and sixty pounds of opium. His haul was worth $4,000, and the 25 percent reward amounted to more than a year's pay, although Whaley would have to share it with his two partners. The seizure brought some even better news, though. Later that afternoon, Morton promoted Whaley to a position as a regular United States customs inspector.

His pay increased to four dollars per day, and Will made a couple of changes to celebrate. Like most of the other inspectors in the custom house, he began sporting a moustache, which would become as brash and flamboyant as its owner. He also changed his shoes, abandoning the leather-bottomed workman's brogans worn by most of the inspection force for a pair with crepe soles. Much more comfortable, the crepe had another benefit—the shoes made no sound on the decks, steel ladders and warehouse floors he now patrolled. Inspector Whaley could move silently on his rounds, as surprised smugglers and crooked customs men were about to discover. As the year drew to a close, the feared Rubber Man, had been born, and Will Whaley was moving on up.

5

HIDDEN HANDS

SILENT PARTNERS

The creation of the great smuggling ring that would one day crown Will Whaley as its king was still three years off in the future. But when Whaley, McLean and Metcalf's creation was born, it would need much more than the talents of those three men to operate successfully. The three were going where no one had gone before, creating a drug trafficking organization, America's first. This would require capital, connections for supplies and transportation and labor to move product from the source country to an eager market in San Francisco. These are all needs familiar to drug traffickers today, but in 1886, the *Halcyon* men were blazing a completely new trail.

Years on the San Francisco waterfront and in Chinatown provided Whaley with some of the necessary contacts and connections, beginning with McLean and Metcalf. As 1886 passed, he and McLean began putting those pieces together. The ring's organizational meetings took place at Whaley's new home in the Baldwin Hotel and at Herman Otterson's saloon off Union Square.

Both Whaley and McLean traveled to Victoria, British Columbia, to meet with investors and the Chinese merchants who had opium for sale, as well as to sort out the distribution end in San Francisco. When they had these men and all the logistics in place, the opium ring would finally complete a full circle.

Baldwin Hotel and Theatre, corner of Powell and Market Streets, Will Whaley's home and headquarters for the opium ring. *Bancroft Library, University of California, Berkeley.*

The Almost Silent Partner

Albert W. Wilson was a little fellow, five and a half feet tall with blue-gray eyes and a dark moustache, a florid complexion and a persistent cough. Born in Balga, East Prussia, in October 1863, he was a mariner by trade, first coming to the United States in 1878 as an ordinary seaman aboard a British ship. Arrested in New South Wales, Australia, in 1883 for stealing a boat and burglary, he moved permanently to America after completing his year in Sydney's notorious Darlinghurst Gaol.

In San Francisco, he changed his name to Wilson, the name he used over the door of his store on Second Street. That's also the name the ex-convict gave the United States Treasury Department in 1887, when he listed himself as the purchaser of the schooner *Halcyon*.

Although Wilson was *Halcyon*'s sole owner on the registration papers, this was a lie, one of a few in the little German's meagre biography. He lived a few doors down from his store and walked the short block from number 29 Second Street to the sporting goods emporium that sold mostly fishing gear to fellow anglers. Wilson fished the bay and the offshore waters outside the Golden Gate, a hobby he shared with another opium ring partner and friend, C.S. Joslyn.

Scrawny and sallow, Wilson's most distinctive characteristic might have been that nagging cough, the most obvious symptom of the wasting disease that would kill him at age thirty-five. Wilson was a "lunger," a victim of the greatest killer in world history. *Mycobacterium tuberculosis*, the bacteria responsible for tuberculosis, the dreaded consumption, has killed billions of humans since the dawn of time, and it still claims nearly two million victims each year.

Known by many names—phthisis, scrofula, consumption, the romantic disease, the white plague—tuberculosis had become, by the 1880s, a scourge across the planet. Born in Africa, it had spread to all continents, infecting, by some estimates, a third of the world's population. In most people, the disease lay dormant—latent tuberculosis—and would go undetected, the carrier blissfully unaware of the infection. In others, a tenth of all those on Earth, or in some decades, like the Gay Nineties in America, as many as a fifth, the symptoms would manifest themselves. Most would see the pulmonary version, a chronic cough, a fever, bloody sputum and the shedding of pounds—the "consumption" that added up to a probable death sentence.

Western author Bob Boze Bell described the awful effects in his book *The Illustrated Life and Times of "Doc" Holliday*:

> *Consumption can go undetected for some good time, especially if the tendency towards denial is followed. Fatigue is more and more pronounced as one's appetite seems to disappear. One feels "out of sorts" and clammy. Periods of fever come and go. One wakes up in the dead of night drenched in sweat. In the morning, choking, coughing, and spitting up, at first watery fluid, later blood and chunks of lung tissue, rack the sufferer. The chest feels as if it were imploding and the pain of it all leads many to alcohol for temporary respite. To crown it all, many thought the illness a result of moral laxity. Compounded with terror of contagion, the consumptive becomes something of a pariah—a "lunger" despised in and for his infirmity.*

Opium could alleviate some of the symptoms, and sufferers turned to medicines like laudanum for relief, but there was no cure, and the terrible toll peaked in the decades just before the turn of the twentieth century. In big port cities like San Francisco, New Orleans and New York, the killer was taking one in every five or six people who died each year.

If those numbers in the regular community were frightening, they were appalling in the smaller, semisecret one made of opium smokers. In the dank, often subterranean, cramped, dirty, fetid places called opium dens, smokers shared communal pipes, and spittoons were provided with the trays of smoking implements. A survey in Formosa (now Taiwan) around the turn of the century found that opium smokers died of tuberculosis at rates three to four times those of the rest of the population and of pneumonia at rates two to three times higher.

Though far from a cure, opium relieved symptoms, and manufacturers of patent and proprietary medicines processed almost all of the 306 tons of opium imported in 1891 into bottles, either as laudanum or as opium derivatives like morphine. There were hundreds of preparations, like Shiloh's Cure for Consumption, Wistar's Balsam and Piso's Cure, all sold over the counter or on a doctor's prescription, and they addicted hundreds of thousands. Without the hopelessness and the dead end of consumption, without the utter inability of doctors to change the course of the underlying disease, America's nineteenth century opium problem might not have happened at all. The coincidence that the great killer of the age was a lung disease and that almost the only medicine in a drugstore that "worked" was opium created the demand that brought millions of pounds of opium into the country.

It would kill lunger Albert W. Wilson, but in 1888, when he was only twenty-five, the front man for the opium ring sold his store and took his case

Advertisement for Piso's Cure for Consumption, which contained alcohol, opium and cannabis. Many such ads of the time depicted children or infants, a subliminal message that the drug was safe for people of all ages. *Author's collection.*

of TB north to Victoria, not completely relocating but moving closer to the opium action, joining with Joslyn, also a part-time resident of Victoria. There, the two of them anchored the northern end of the business as they watched *Halcyon* come and go.

The Wharf Rat

Albion J. Smith was born just north of Arcata in Crescent City, California, in February 1861, making him roughly the same age as his future partner, Will Whaley. In 1877, he moved down the coast to San Francisco, landing a good job in the city clerking for Alfred Metcalf's old outfit, Goodall, Nelson, & Perkins.

A freight clerk met just about everybody in the shipping business at his wharf, including the ships' crews, the longshoremen, the freight haulers, the cargo owners and of course the customs men, and they were perfectly positioned to help smugglers. Another clerk, Henry L. Foss, ran a successful scheme from the Oceanic pier for years before being caught, but A.J. Smith did it first, running untaxed opium across Broadway Wharf for more than a decade before his bosses at Goodall, Nelson, and the Pacific Coast Steamship Service (PCSS) decided they'd had enough.

By the time Smith left in 1887, he had acquired a tugboat, a ranch and other properties, as well as all of the contacts he needed to help his new partners in the opium ring. He knew people, including Alfred Metcalf, and some of the customs men, too, as the wharf handled trade from ports in Canada, San Francisco's prime source for opium.

He also worked with pursers Charles Joslyn of the SS *Idaho* and Frank J. Curtin of the SS *Umatilla*, both regulars on the Victoria run. Pursers weren't responsible for the ship's cargo, but they did sometimes keep the records of freight carried on the line's passenger steamers, along with the passenger manifest and other papers for the voyage. In any case, a freight clerk and a purser made a great team. Add a customs inspector who could stick a "passed" label onto the package or the crate, and it was a recipe for success and prosperity.

Smith's PCSS employers eventually fired him, not for opium smuggling but for a shortage in his accounts, and Smith paid back the money with the proceeds of the sale of his tugboat and some ranch land. This saved him from criminal charges but left the unemployed Smith free to pursue his new

Left: Albion J. Smith, financial backer for the opium ring. *National Archives.*

Below: Broadway Wharf at the foot of Broadway in San Francisco, home to the Pacific Coast Steamship Service and workplace for freight clerk A.J. Smith. *University of California, Berkeley.*

career as an opium smuggler with Will Whaley and Ewen McLean. The day would come, though, when the wharf rat would turn, and when that day came, he would shatter the opium ring forever.

6
THE PRINCE AND THE DIPLOMAT

The Man Who Saw the Elephant

One of the older and certainly the most experienced members of the *Halcyon* ring, Charles Sumner Joslyn, was born in Batavia, New York, in June 1838. Like Will Whaley, he was a big man, about six feet tall, with an outsized, forceful personality to go with it. Joslyn's father was a shoemaker, and one of his brothers would go into the family business, but Charles chose a different course, moving from Batavia to work as a bookkeeper in New York City at twenty-one, while looking for even broader horizons. He got a passport in July 1860, taking the first of many hundreds of sea voyages in August, traveling to England aboard the SS *Adriatic*.

The Civil War brought him home, and he answered the call to duty, enlisting on July 3, 1861, just before the First Battle of Bull Run. Mustering in as a private in the Fifth New York Volunteer Infantry Regiment, he left the army as a sergeant major after seeing action at the Battles of Antietam, South Mountain and Second Bull Run.

After his Civil War experience, Joslyn returned to New York City, working as a broker before moving into the civil service. He joined the crony-filled customs house as a clerk in January 1871, hired by collector Thomas Murphy, a Tammany Hall politician and confederate of powerful New York senator Roscoe Conkling. Joslyn's stint at customs ended when Murphy lost his job in a political putsch in the scandal-plagued administration of President Ulysses S. Grant.

Charles Sumner Joslyn, "Boss Harris," opium smuggler, financier and purser on ships of the Pacific Coast Steamship Service. *Impression from the* Chicago Tribune, *October 1889.*

Still a young man in his late twenties and unattached, Joslyn chose to make the break—a big one—taking himself all the way across the continent to San Francisco to a new set of opportunities. He caught on immediately with the Pacific Mail Steamship Company, one of the oldest and largest shipping lines in the Pacific and a major player in the California merchant trade. Joslyn took the position of purser on the SS *Alaska*, a big paddlewheel steamer, on the transpacific route to Hong Kong and was aboard when the Great Hong Kong Typhoon of September 1874 caught *Alaska* and threw it ashore, Joslyn's first shipwreck.

In constant contact with merchants and businessmen ashore, the captain, officers and crew, the purser was the best-connected person on the ship. The purser was also responsible for maintaining the passenger manifest and collected the customs declarations for presentation to the inspectors who boarded the vessel when it arrived in port. A former customs man himself, Joslyn was comfortable with the procedure and, over the course of twenty years and several hundred voyages, met and dealt with plenty of inspectors.

And the Pacific Mail Steamship Service was the perfect vehicle for smuggling. The PMSS ships moved down the Pacific coast to Panama and Chile, out to Fiji and Australia and to Honolulu, Japan, China and Hong Kong. The Pacific Mail operated as close to a clockwork schedule as was possible at the time, with San Francisco as its American hub. Coal-powered with sails for backup, the PMSS steamers kept to a regular timetable and moved cargo and passengers reliably and (mostly) safely to the western end of America's transcontinental railroad. PMSS ships ferried thousands of Chinese immigrants to the United States before the Chinese Exclusion Act shut down this lucrative business in 1882.

Over the next few years, Joslyn served on more than half a dozen of the Pacific Mail's finest ships, and these long voyages to foreign points gave him plenty of opportunities to make useful contacts and smuggle shipments of opium and other goods.

In 1882, Joslyn married Elise Fruchtnicht of Napa, a German woman and transplanted New Yorker like himself, and he changed employers that same year, leaving the Pacific Mail and going to another local company, the Pacific Coast Steamship Company. The PCSS wasn't a rival of the Pacific Mail but instead focused on the coast, which meant no more long voyages to Hong Kong and Sydney. Sailing from the Broadway Wharf, Joslyn's new ship, the SS *Idaho*, made an eleven-day run to Sitka, Alaska, via Nanaimo and Victoria, British Columbia. Instead of being gone for two months or more at a time, Joslyn would now be away for three weeks.

The Chinese Exclusion Act went into effect in 1882, so any Chinese people who wanted to get into the United States after passage of the law were obliged to use the back door, not the golden one that Emma Lazarus had waxed so poetic about. On the West Coast, that back door opened from British Columbia, Canada, with enterprising human traffickers sneaking Chinese immigrants down through Puget Sound into Washington.

At almost exactly the same moment, Congress took a look at the customs tariffs and decided that the federal government wasn't making enough money from certain items, one of which was "opium prepared for smoking." In one of those little acts full of unintended consequences, the lawmakers boosted the customs duties on smoking opium by four dollars per pound,

Chinese immigrants aboard the SS *Alaska*, 1876. C.S. Joslyn was a purser aboard this Pacific Mail steamship at the time and responsible for all of the passengers, including the Chinese. Harper's Weekly, *Smithsonian Institution Libraries.*

effective January 1, 1884. An observer from 2021 could make the argument that the war on drugs started with that decision and on that date.

The smuggling certainly did. Customs inspectors like Will Whaley made regular seizures on the PMSS steamers coming from Hong Kong and from the other ships on the Asia runs. Smoking opium had been selling for around ten to twelve dollars per pound in San Francisco, so the increase in the duty effectively doubled the price. The Chinatown merchants, knowing it was coming, stocked up in advance at the six-dollar duty in 1883, shipping only a half-ton in all of 1884. At least forty more tons were being smuggled into the country, the bulk of it coming due south from British Columbia.

Now Joslyn had PCSS ships on the same Victoria to San Francisco run. After 1884, Victoria became the opium capital of North America, receiving, processing and trans-shipping hundreds of tons of the drug, all of it destined for the United States. Joslyn, with his excellent connections in San Francisco, on the ships, and now in Victoria, too, quickly became the go-to man in the opium trade. He even got a nickname, "Boss Harris," and he set up not just his own loads for San Francisco but also shipments for others.

Joslyn's smuggling partners included the captain of his own ship, the SS *Idaho*, James C. "Jimmy" Carroll. A seizure at Port Townsend in December 1885 sent customs officials to Kasaan Bay, Alaska, where they found 3,112 pounds of opium at a salting plant leased by Carroll. He'd gotten the opium through Joslyn's connections in Victoria. The newspapers noted that it was the largest opium seizure ever made in the United States, valued at $45,000 at the going rate of $15 per pound ($1.2 million in 2019 dollars). It might still hold the record.

The officers never connected Joslyn to the shipment, and he was still in the opium business in 1888, when the *Chicago Tribune* got onto a story about smuggling into the Midwest. The article identified him by his Boss Harris nickname, describing him as a millionaire and "fantastically wealthy" from his dealings in the smuggling trade. When the story was written, Joslyn had taken his experience, contacts and money and partnered with the men of the schooner *Halcyon*. The era of the amateur smuggler wasn't entirely over; passengers and crewmen would still try their luck and are still doing so today. But game was changing, and the professionals were taking over.

When Whaley and McLean arrived in Victoria, they immediately turned to the man who had connections to every opium seller and smuggler in Canada. Charles Joslyn, the man newspapers called the "Prince of Smugglers," was only too happy to help.

Diplomat and Pineapple King

At the Sparta Restaurant and Saloon on the corner of Sansome and Merchant Streets, a flock of Greek waiters carried some of the city's finest dishes to San Francisco's elite. The Sparta, known for its Italian chef and its old-world charm, hosted many banquets and lavish dinners in its large dining rooms over the years, and countless business meetings as well. It was in the private offices on the second floor that the Sparta's owner conducted his own business. There, he and his brother ran the restaurant and their wholesale fruit sales operation next door. And there they hosted some cohorts who wanted to keep things a little more confidential. This included the men of the opium ring.

The Sparta sat almost in the shadow of the United States Appraiser's Building, just across the street. The assistant U.S. attorneys, deputy marshals, Secret Service agents and Treasury special agent Joseph Evans ate at the Sparta occasionally. Demetrius G. "Cammy" Camarinos ran the restaurant, and the California Fruit Market moved next door from the corner of Sutter and Powell Streets. Camarinos cut a fine figure in San Francisco, the picture of prosperity and, at least in the city's small Greek community, power.

He emigrated from Sparta, Greece, in 1877, making it all the way to San Francisco the following year. Although he was college educated in Greece, his English wasn't great, and he started humbly as a dishwasher in a coffee shop. That didn't last, as Cammy bought the fruit store the very next year, and he had his fingers in some other pies. His brother Panagiotis, who went by Peter, came to town to help with the store in 1887, but the two of them had a vision, and it involved fruit and Hawaii.

D. G. Camarinos.

Demetrius G. Camarinos, Greek businessman in San Francisco and Honolulu. His Sparta Restaurant at Sansome and Merchant Streets served as headquarters for the opium ring. San Francisco Chronicle.

In a move that would have important ramifications for the opium side of the business, Peter headed to the islands to check things out and immediately opened a Honolulu branch of the store. The California Fruit Market, at the corner of King and Alakea Streets, just a block from the Iolani Palace, became an immediate success, selling fruits, vegetables, fish and other edibles shipped from California aboard the four Oceanic steamships. That was half the vision, as those same ships then loaded up with Hawaiian fruits, mangoes, papayas, bananas and pineapple, especially after Camarinos installed refrigerated containers aboard all four ships. From 1887 on, every one of those liners sailed from Honolulu or San Francisco with Camarinos's fruit, meats and produce aboard.

Back on the mainland, business took off, and Cammy moved to the larger quarters on Sansome Street. By that time, he had made friends with some of the customs men and with two former employees, William A. Whaley and Ewen W. McLean. Camarinos used his businesses to launder the money from smuggling, plowing opium and fruit profits into a growing conglomerate. With wealth came power, and the Greek government appointed Camarinos as its acting San Francisco consul in 1892, giving him even more prominence and some diplomatic immunity.

Peter spent most of his time in Honolulu, where both the opium and fruit businesses prospered, and a new fruit, pineapple, showed real promise. The brothers set up the Pearl City Fruit Company, invested heavily in plantation acreages for growing pineapple, and experimented with different strains. By 1893, Camarinos was one of the two largest pineapple growers in Hawaii, shipping the very popular fruit regularly on the Oceanic steamers to California.

Pineapple grew into Hawaii's second-largest industry behind sugar, with thousands of acres on the islands—and later, the entire island of Lanai—planted with the fruit. The business owed a large part of its success to pineapple pioneers Peter and Demetrius Camarinos—and to the opium money that financed them.

Cammy's San Francisco connections included another Spartan, George Lycurgus, who had come to the city and established a restaurant as the Greek community grew. The high-profile Lycurgus was comfortable in every social setting, working with the Chinese, Greeks and with some of San Francisco's leading citizens. This included Claus Spreckels, one of the brothers who owned *Halcyon*'s old racing rival, *Lurline*. Spreckels headed a vast empire in California and Hawaii, built on sugar, shipping and banking. At one point, Spreckels owned the largest sugar cane plantation in the world, creating a town, Spreckelsville, on Maui for his workers. He also held a sizable portion of Hawaii's debt and quite a bit of King Kalakaua's personal liabilities.

Lycurgus played poker with the Sugar King and claimed that in one 1886 game aboard a Hawaii-bound steamer, Spreckels and his playing partners kept the amiable Greek distracted until after the ship sailed from San

George Lycurgus traveled to Hawaii in 1889 with William Whaley, setting up the *Halcyon* ring's most important smuggling run. *Wikipedia Commons.*

Francisco. That practical joke and involuntary voyage was the first of many for Lycurgus, who made himself at home in Hawaii.

Thanks to Spreckels's contacts, Lycurgus met David Kalakaua and became a poker buddy right off. He joined Peter Camarinos in a couple of fruit businesses, leasing twenty acres of land behind Honolulu in Manoa Valley to grow bananas and more acreage up the coast in Waianae. A shareholder in Camarinos's Pearl City Fruit Company, Lycurgus had a hand in several restaurants over the years, plus a stint as the owner of a hotel, the Sans Souci, located at the end of Waikiki Beach. Author Robert Louis Stevenson stayed at the Sans Souci, and the hotel was profitable enough that Lycurgus could invest in other ventures, including opium.

Lycurgus knew Whaley from San Francisco, and he became a partner in the *Halcyon*'s smuggling operations, urging Whaley to tap the Hawaii market, where the prices per tin could triple those in San Francisco. In time, he and Whaley would travel to Honolulu to check out the possibilities, with Lycurgus giving Whaley the grand tour and introducing him to friends who could be helpful in a smuggling venture. With Greek help, the conspiracy spun up, and with everyone on board, the opium ring was finally complete.

7

FROM CUSTOMS OFFICER TO KING OF THE OPIUM RING

Although the *Halcyon* conspirators came to their agreement in December 1886 and didn't begin shipping opium for another five months, the market conditions that made the project viable had been put in place four years earlier, when Will Whaley, the Rubber Man, was still working for the customs service. In 1882, Congress raised the six-dollar-per-pound tariff on smoking opium to ten dollars, the change taking effect on January 1 and drastically altering the market.

Everyone knew it was coming, and the Chinese merchants of San Francisco went on a buying spree, shipping a whopping 298,152 pounds of smoking opium through American ports in 1882, most of it toward the end of the year. Fully stocked up, legal imports totaled only 1,066 pounds in 1883. Everyone also knew that after January 1, smuggling would increase, and that prices in town would go up to reflect the new costs of doing business.

In San Francisco, Will Whaley and the other inspectors greeted 1883 with renewed enthusiasm. In March, Whaley was part of an inspection team that searched the steamer *Arabic* again, the process lasting almost three days. The team moved methodically through the vessel, searching compartments and putting customs seals on the hatches of the spaces already cleared. Most of the first two days had been unproductive; Whaley found two and a half pounds of opium and five cloth coats, all undeclared but with a total value of only sixty-two dollars.

At 5:00 p.m. on March 28, the inspection crew went off duty, but the Rubber Man, still suspicious, remained behind, lurking in the dark spaces between decks, where he observed some of the Chinese crewmen breaking the seals on a hatchway leading to a coal bunker. Apprehending the sailors, Whaley hit the jackpot under the coal, finding twenty silk coats, sixteen cloth coats, fifty-five serge coats, ten cotton coats, 520 silk handkerchiefs and twelve silk dress patterns. Whaley's share of the $1,000 seizure came to $250, almost three months' pay for the inspector. A newspaper editor commented that this had been "very good work for the customs officers," but in fact it was a credit to the Rubber Man, whose persistence had again paid off handsomely.

He scored again on July 12, 1883, after becoming suspicious of a gang of stevedores shifting cargo from the SS *Coptic*. The steamer, just in from Hong Kong and Yokohama, was tied up at the Pacific Mail wharf. The Rubber Man's instincts were right. Stopping Daniel Connors at the foot of the gangway, he searched the longshoreman, discovering eight pounds of crude opium concealed under wrappings around Connors's torso, waist and legs. Although Connors "tried hard to give off and pleaded poverty and a large family," Whaley arrested him on the spot. The U.S. marshal held Connors on $500 bail, and Whaley received a quarter of the value of his $100 seizure.

Inspector James Rourke, Daniel Connors and the unnamed Chinese sailors from the *Arabic* had been unlucky. Caught red-handed, they were arrested and sent before a federal judge for trial. Rourke was convicted and got a short sentence in the county jail. Most, like Connors, received a small fine, but many other seizures like the one from the massive PMSS liner SS *City of Peking* on November 8, 1883, could not be linked to anyone.

One of the largest ships in the world, the *City of Peking* carried passengers and freight from Hong Kong and Yokohama, its regularly scheduled transpacific route. Whaley and his crew boarded the ship that morning and spent much of the day going over the ship without much success. In the afternoon, however, Whaley decided to search a box stringer, a hollow support beam that ran almost the entire length of the 423-foot ship. The stringer was much too confined for a big man like Whaley, 5-foot-11 and over two hundred pounds, or even for the smaller men in the inspection team, so Whaley went onto the wharf and found a small boy willing to venture almost one hundred yards down the tunnel. He backed out again with more than thirty pounds of opium valued at over $400, and Whaley shared some of the $100 reward with the "little fellow" who had helped him.

On August 12, 1884, Whaley scored again on the SS *Arabic*, discovering nine pounds of opium hidden under a locker in the passenger compartment.

SS *City of Peking*, sister to the *City of Tokio* and one of the largest steamships in the world. The site of another Whaley opium seizure. *Library of Congress.*

Because the contraband had been hidden in an area that housed the "steerage" or lowest class of passengers, the smugglers could have been from among any of the crew or the passengers, so no arrests were possible. As usual, the opium, valued at over $100, was auctioned off, with Whaley receiving the 25 percent commission, the equivalent of a week's pay.

Most of the schemes to move contraband weren't very sophisticated, and some were almost impromptu. Haberdashery caused the downfall of more than one smuggler on the Embarcadero. On October 8, 1883, Quartermaster Peter Matson of the SS *City of Peking*, his hat jauntily perched atop his head, strolled down the gangplank from the liner to the PMSS wharf. Will Whaley was waiting and suspicious of the sailor's headgear. He tilted it to find two five-tael tins of opium underneath. Whaley arrested Matson and turned him over to the U.S. marshal. In another incident that caused great amusement among the customs inspectors, a polite but clearly distracted young gentleman tipped his own hat to a passing lady, revealing the tin of opium underneath.

The inspectors confronted these and dozens of other attempts every day, the Rubber Man racking up seizures at an impressive rate. He and his adversaries were playing a very old, and by now a very familiar game, and Whaley was learning it by heart. And it *was* a game for the most part—not the high stakes, life-or-death struggle that the war on drugs has become today. Opium smugglers in 1883 mostly risked a fifty-dollar fine, and many cases were never filed or were dismissed by the United States attorney before trial.

Even if it wanted to, the federal government had no agency set up to investigate even big seizures like the one from the *City of Tokio*. The Treasury

Department had two special agents in San Francisco. On the lookout for smuggling and possible corruption in the customs force, they were Republican political appointees like the rest of the high-ranking customs staff, and more mundane duties like preparing reports on glove imports and monitoring immigration kept the special agents busy.

So, the heaviest burden fell on Whaley and the other inspectors at the point where the ships entered San Francisco Bay, and where about fifty of these men had to work on up to a dozen ships entering the port every day of the week. Not all of the ships arrived from foreign destinations, so the inspectors could concentrate their efforts on the ones that were likeliest to have dutiable merchandise aboard. At Meiggs Wharf, before the ship touched land or any local vessel touched it, a team of the surveyor's men went aboard. At this first contact, the captain or the purser produced the ship's papers, reported any disease on board and turned over the passenger and cargo manifests and the crew list. Customs collected declarations from everyone aboard, and inspectors interviewed and searched the passengers and their luggage. Others began searching the entire ship and all of its hundreds of potential hiding places, looking for items that might have been concealed.

Ships such as the *City of Tokio*, five thousand tons and 423 feet long, or the *Mariposa*, a little smaller at 314 feet and three thousand tons, had thousands of nooks and crannies where things of value could be hidden. The crewmen, who knew their ship intimately, had found all of these places, and they were the ones who were being well paid to hide opium tins or silk handkerchiefs or whatever the smugglers wanted smuggled. After years of playing the game, the customs inspectors knew most of the hiding places, too, and saw many of these ships on a routine basis, checking ships like the *Coptic*, *Arabic* and *City of Tokio* carefully when they arrived.

This search was a dirty, unpleasant and occasionally dangerous task. Doing a thorough job meant crawling through dark, dank, filthy holes in the company of rats and insects, checking wastewater tanks and the bilges of ships and facing the same risks on the water that sailors confronted. In 1882, Captain J.D. Malcstedt, Whaley's watch commander of the night inspection force, fell from the deck of the steamer *Gaelic*, striking his head against a fender and suffering "excessive internal concussions." He would recover, but inspector John M. Plunkett was killed on San Francisco Bay on July 2, 1897, when a tugboat he was aboard ran into an anchored scow schooner. Other officers drowned, got blown up or were killed in gunfights on the border, and some had their health ruined by exposure in winter conditions or to the hazardous materials they inspected. The government

Customs officers inspecting arriving Chinese immigrants at San Francisco. Harper's Weekly Magazine, *1875.*

did not pay workers comp or provide sick leave. These risks, too, were all part of the game.

If the inspectors found anything, the game was usually over right there. Seized opium or other goods were taken from the ship to the Custom House, turned over to the U.S. marshal and sold at auction on the steps of the U.S. Courthouse. The seizing officer collected his 25 percent, and everybody but the smuggler went home happy.

There was another part of the game, one that almost everyone played with a wink and a nod and cash changing hands in exchange for an inspector's failure to find something the government paid him four dollars per day to seek out. These bribes, there is no politer term, might be impromptu, arranged on the spot between a passenger or crewman whose opium was just discovered and an inspector with a flexible attitude toward official corruption. In some cases, the arrangements might be made in advance; inspectors would be told of a large shipment, told to not search in certain spaces and were well rewarded for their diligence or lack thereof. Having an inspector in their pockets or, better yet, a lieutenant or an assistant to the surveyor made smuggling much easier for the opium merchants of Chinatown. Bribery made the opium game possible. Some did better at the game than others.

Will Whaley played quite well. The service kept an accurate record of his seizures and the reward money paid to him, and by 1885, statistically speaking, he was the most successful inspector in San Francisco and possibly the entire United States. But something was happening behind the efficient, effective, official façade of customs inspector William A. Whaley. In 1885, he got his second promotion—assistant to the surveyor of the port, a position that gave him a raise in pay to $1,800 annually. The Rubber Man, after only three years on the job, was making $300 per year more than his father, who had been working for Treasury almost since Will was born.

Whaley's new job gave him leeway to choose his assignments and pick out the choicest ships with the most lucrative seizure and reward opportunities. These were, of course, the same ones that came with the richest bribe opportunities, and there was plenty of evidence that Will Whaley had already started down that dark road.

He moved from modest lodgings at 1100 Van Ness Avenue to somewhat better digs at the Parker House, 1122 Market Street, but he was doing a lot of entertaining at the even fancier, more luxurious Baldwin Hotel, located at Powell and Market. And San Francisco's carriage trade had taken to spending its Sundays on pleasant jaunts to the posh and pricey Cliff House restaurant, out on the headland overlooking the Golden Gate. Well dressed and fitting right in, Will Whaley made those Cliff House Sundays a regular stop on his social schedule. William Whaley had just turned twenty-four years old.

8

RED EAGLE AND THE LONG ARM OF THE LAW

Someone noticed Whaley's suspiciously improved circumstances, because in 1885, not long after Will Whaley's promotion, customs fired its ace employee. President Grover Cleveland was inaugurated for the first of his two nonconsecutive terms that March, and the Democrat did some presidential housecleaning of Republican political appointees. In San Francisco, Cleveland selected John S. Hager as collector of customs, and Hager promptly seized Ewen McLean's Hawaiian opium while he did some scrubbing of his own. He started with his Chinese translator. John Morton, the port surveyor and William Whaley's mentor and immediate boss, was out too. A number of other customs officials resigned or left involuntarily, and the carnage extended down into the inspector ranks.

Some of this was due to the continuing fallout from the *City of Tokio* case, but another scandal was heating up—one that was closer to home and much more recent. If collector Hager and his new surveyor were comforted to hear that this scandal, at least, didn't have anything to do with opium, their relief didn't last. November saw almost a dozen of Hager's former employees glumly lined up on wooden benches outside the federal grand jury room, waiting their turns to testify about Chinese immigrants—hundreds and possibly thousands of them—had walked right through U.S. Customs in San Francisco over the past several years.

Will Whaley and Ewen McLean, both former customs employees, had a taste of the good life in the past couple of years and were not ready to give it up. The very profitable human trafficking scheme they'd been running was as dead as Abraham Lincoln. It wouldn't work without insiders at customs, and all but one of the insiders were sitting right there on the grand jury bench, their access gone forever. That left opium, and the idea for the country's first drug trafficking organization started with the two men outside the courtroom.

Whaley, formerly the smugglers' nemesis in San Francisco, thought he had found a better way. Getting a few tins or a couple of hundred past the inspectors was slow, chancy and inefficient. And hiding four thousand tins on a ship, even one as big as the *City of Tokio*, was asking for trouble. Whaley wanted his own ship, one that was fast enough to beat the revenue cutters and could land the opium anywhere along California's 840 miles of almost empty coastline.

While Whaley looked for a ship, captain and crew, McLean, the bookkeeper, dealt with the other problems—finding a source of supply, customers and financing. He knew the insatiable demand in Chinatown and that there was an unlimited supply of opium in British Columbia and Hong Kong, and he and Whaley set out to connect the two.

The plan wouldn't come together for another year. Before it did, they had to deal with the fallout—a grand jury investigation and a couple of trials—from their last scheme, the very successful human trafficking operation that relied on a hole in America's anti-Chinese wall. Congress created the hole, Section 6 of the Chinese Exclusion Act of 1882, which permitted Chinese people already lawfully in the United States to leave the country and come back. To do so, they obtained a certificate that would be presented to the customs inspector when they returned. Printed on pink paper with an eagle at the top, these Section 6 certificates were known in San Francisco as "Red Eagles."

Many of the Chinese men who were traveling to China had no intention of returning to America and no longer needed their papers. Thousands in Hong Kong and China did want the Red Eagle certificates and were willing to pay handsomely for them, and in 1883, two customs men tapped that market.

Customs stamp affixed to every half-pound (five-tael) tin of imported smoking opium. This is from the SS *Romulus* at San Francisco, September 8, 1893. *Author's collection.*

Ferdinand Ciprico, customs inspector convicted in the Red Eagle immigration fraud cases. *San Quentin inmate photo, California State Library.*

Ferdinand Ciprico started his customs career as a night inspector working the midnight shift in 1882 with William Whaley. The burly officer with a walrus moustache and dark, droopy eyes now worked in the registration section interviewing returning Chinese residents with his partner, William "Champagne Billy" Boyd. Dark-haired, handsome and with a waxed moustache, Boyd had a way with the women and a taste for high living. Neither spoke Chinese, so they joined with part-time customs translator Ewen W. McLean to do the interviews, and McLean brought in his partner, Will Whaley.

Boyd obtained thousands of real certificates and sent them to China with insurance salesman Adolph Hinz, who lined up customers in Hong Kong. Demand was ferocious, and soon, hundreds were arriving at the port. There, Ciprico and McLean did the interviews, verified the certificates and admitted the bearers to the United States. The money poured in.

The scheme hummed along smoothly for at least a year before other customs employees got suspicious and reported problems with some of the supposedly returning Chinese people. Collector Hager fired his four employees, and the case went to the Treasury agents for an investigation that would last almost two years before a grand jury indicted McLean, Whaley and the others in late 1887. The evidence against the group included lurid tales of big spending and lavish excess by the conspirators. One story that became legend told of a wild party at the Baldwin Hotel, Whaley's residence, where Billy Boyd bought enough champagne, $1,800 worth, to give his current mistress a bath in the bubbly.

Even with this evidence, the case had problems. Boyd fled to Australia with over $60,000 in cash. Prosecutors made a deal with Hinz, but he was a bad witness, and the evidence against Whaley was very weak. At trial in early 1888, even the testimony of Billy Boyd, who returned to make a deal, could not convince a jury that acquitted McLean and hung up on Ciprico. The U.S. attorney dropped all charges against Whaley, and he and McLean returned to their new interest, smuggling opium. The Red Eagle conspiracy placed Whaley and McLean firmly on the road to crime and put them there together, smuggling opium in *Halcyon* as Whaley fitted himself for the crown of King of the Opium Ring.

9

BY THE LIGHT OF THE MOON

In 1888, the dozen opium factories in Victoria, British Columbia, turned out over 90,000 pounds of smoking opium. By 1891, the number reached 125,311 pounds, and an enterprising reporter from the *New York Herald* went west to see if anyone knew where all of that opium had gone. A Canadian Customs official had the answer. "'It was smuggled into the United States,' he responded in an offhand way."

Victoria is only a few days' sailing for a fast little ship like Metcalf's schooner. In 1887, the capital of British Columbia was still a small town of about twelve thousand, a fraction of whom were Chinese, much too small of a market to consume the thirty-three tons of opium imported that year. The Pacific Coast Steamship Company provided British Columbia with regular steamer service, ships like the SS *Umatilla* and C.S. Joslyn's *Idaho* each, making the trip to the big market in San Francisco every couple of weeks. Many of them reported opium on the cargo manifest, and most carried more somewhere on board that went undeclared. *Idaho* was notorious for it.

When Will Whaley and Ewen McLean arrived in Victoria in 1886, they found merchants like Sing Wo Chan offering opium "in any quantity required" in the *Victoria Daily Colonist*. Moving into the Driard Hotel, Victoria's best at the time, the two smugglers began organizing the Canadian end of their new business.

Ad hoc and disorganized smuggling operations continued. Ship's officers, crewmen and passengers carried small quantities south, hoping to get their tins through customs undetected, or used small boats to move opium and

Bird's-eye view of Victoria, British Columbia, 1889. *Library of Congress.*

immigrants south to Seattle, Tacoma or Port Townsend. The revenue men knew all about their opponents, as informants in Victoria, hoping for rewards, reported smugglers' movements, but customs had nothing larger than a rowboat on Puget Sound and the bigger revenue cutters, *Bear*, *Corwin* and *Rush*, were usually in Alaskan waters or in California. The smaller, slower USRC *Oliver Wolcott*, based at Port Townsend, had little luck catching the speedy little boats carrying contraband and undocumented Chinese immigrants.

In Victoria, C.S. Joslyn facilitated smuggling at both ends of the traffic. Operating from a modest house at 141 Chatham Street, just north and east of Chinatown, Joslyn, who listed himself in Victoria's city directory as a "capitalist," had connections throughout the city and spread out through Canada and the eastern United States. Joslyn didn't speak Chinese, but he had excellent relationships with the local opium merchants, particularly Lee Hong of the Bow Yuen Company and Tai Soong and Co., both of which refined the crude opium into the smokable version and sold it in quantity.

The Chinese population of Canada was much smaller than that of the United States. The 1881 census found only 4,383, with 99.2 percent living in British Columbia. By 1891, that number more than doubled to 9,129, still perhaps only a third of the number of Chinese people in the San Francisco Bay area alone. As in the United States, most of these Chinese Canadians—97 percent—were male, and about 2,500 lived in Victoria, the provincial capital and main commercial center. Victoria was the key link in the trade, with maritime connections to Hong Kong, Honolulu and San

Francisco, and the opium factories on Cormorant and Government Streets selling processed opium and refining the crude form before packaging it for resale and shipment into the United States.

Whaley and McLean traveled to Victoria at least three times in 1886 and 1887, setting up their opium ring even before *Halcyon* was ready to sail. In August 1887, Metcalf brought the ship north, not to Victoria, where Whaley was waiting, but to a protected inlet a few miles west of the city. Whaley hired a local boat to carry the opium to Sooke—1,600 pounds concealed in boxes marked "coal oil," all that he had been able to obtain for this first run. Although *Halcyon* lingered at Sooke for ten days, no more opium was forthcoming, and Metcalf upped anchor and set sail, arriving at Drake's Bay after four days.

The offload crew, Jack Gallagher and a Greek man named Manuel, came out disguised as fishermen in a smaller boat named *Flora*, meeting *Halcyon* offshore in the wide bay south of Point Reyes. Named for Sir Francis Drake, who called there in 1579, and now part of the Point Reyes National Seashore, the area is largely unspoiled today and looks much like it did in 1887, with a shingled beach at the base of white cliffs that curve in a ten-mile arc.

About thirty miles north of San Francisco, the bay was near enough to the city to be convenient and far from both the customs officers, who seldom patrolled outside the Golden Gate, and the revenue cutters, which were all up in Alaska. Whaley told Metcalf to hover outside the bay and then use *Halcyon*'s small boat to run the opium to the beach. Safely ashore, Manuel and Jack would move the cargo by wagon over the San Bruno Road to the San Francisco Bay side of the peninsula. There, *Flora* or another vessel at one of the Marin County waterfront towns—Sausalito or

Tai Soong Company, Cormorant Street, Victoria, refined and supplied opium to Joslyn, Whaley and the *Halcyon* ring. *Archives of British Columbia.*

Chinese abalone man at Drakes Bay, *Halcyon*'s California rendezvous point. *Stereoview card, author's collection.*

San Rafael—would be waiting to take the opium down to San Francisco. Whaley and Metcalf sorted out problems with the first loads, but by the end of the year, the operation was proceeding smoothly, and the money was rolling in.

Halcyon landed loads of 2,400 pounds, 1,900 pounds and another ton on its first three trips, with Whaley aboard for the first run, and McLean buying the opium for $6 per pound in Canada and selling it for double that in San Francisco. It didn't always go smoothly; on one voyage, *Halcyon* had to loiter offshore for six weeks, sailing outside territorial waters during the day and then slipping inshore at night. With profits of $12,000 or more on each load, Whaley managed three trips before the winter storms put an end to the smuggling season for the year and Metcalf laid *Halcyon* up at Antioch from November to February 1888.

As the criminal trial in the Red Eagle certificate case approached in early April, Whaley and McLean needed to be in San Francisco for court, not cruising on the high seas or living it up in Victoria. *Halcyon* made some runs without Whaley aboard in the early months of the year, and then, with the ship becoming more notorious, he tried misdirection, putting out word that *Halcyon* had become a sealer.

Metcalf tried to make the deception work, bringing *Halcyon* into Victoria in early April 1888 with seventeen seal skins aboard. The flimsy cover story didn't hold up; *Halcyon* had none of the usual sealing gear or a hunter on board, and the waterfront touts said that Metcalf had bought the skins from another sealer. When *Halcyon* went back to sea a few days later, nobody thought it was headed toward the Aleutians or Japan.

It wasn't. A week later, the ship turned up in San Francisco, where the customs men gave it a good going over but failed to find either opium or seal skins. McLean told interested reporters that he planned to put the schooner up for sale up in Victoria, and *Halcyon* sailed again on April 20. *Halcyon* arrived at Victoria on May 8, but instead of going on the block, Whaley and Metcalf began fitting it out for what did look like a hunting expedition.

Metcalf picked up a mate, Johnny Cotsford, who actually had some sealing experience. He also got a crew that clamored for berths, thinking they saw through the ruse and signing up for what they believed would be an opium cruise and all its profits. Metcalf surprised his new crew and everyone else on May 23 by turning north out of Victoria, making for the sealing grounds.

The trip flopped, and *Halcyon* returned on September 4 with a few skins and a crew so disgruntled that some of them had deserted in Alaska when they got a chance. This left little enough time in the 1888 season to get back to the real business at hand. Whaley and McLean, back in Victoria after the trial, organized a couple of quick runs down the coast before the weather shut them down.

"A long, low, rakish craft, smuggler *Halcyon*, a newspaper artist's impression. *From the* San Francisco Examiner, *1892.*

Whaley abandoned all pretense in 1889, and *Halcyon* was a smuggler once more. The ring had some trouble getting a crew at the beginning of the season; nobody in Victoria wanted to go sealing with Alfred Metcalf again, and he got a new mate, Dave Laing, but seamen were harder to come by. Whaley eventually talked some Native Americans from Puget Sound into signing on for the first voyage, but an early March trip didn't go well. Missed connections meant *Halcyon* had to return to Canada with its shipment of "coal oil" still aboard. Things settled down after the first glitch-filled trip, and the schooner made a number of successful runs down the coast for the rest of the year.

When Metcalf put into port after one of these trips on September 16, he got some new orders. Whaley wanted *Halcyon* ready for a much longer voyage, a run to Hawaii, and the opium king headed to the islands to check things out on October 18 with Camarinos's friend George Lycurgus. With newspaper men and everyone else watching *Halcyon*'s movements with great interest, Metcalf laid the ship up at Victoria for the winter to await instructions. In late 1889, he got them. The ring that had changed the face of the opium business in San Francisco set its sights on an a distant—and golden—shore. William Whaley and *Halcyon* were bound for Hawaii, and the opium merchants of the kingdom were ready for them.

10

DOPE IN PARADISE

The use of opium is on the increase among the native population of these Islands. The example of another race, coming more and more in contact with the people, produces this result. It is much to be regretted, but nevertheless too true, that the opium pipe may often be seen in the hands of young natives of both sexes.

When the Board of Health wrote those words in 1872, Hawaii had a Chinese population of two thousand and a bustling Chinatown in Honolulu. Although similar in many respects, there were some key differences between the Hawaii and California Chinese immigration situations. Almost all of the immigrants in both countries hailed from the southeastern area of China around Canton, Hong Kong, the Pearl River Delta, Kwangtung and Fujian Provinces. They mostly spoke Cantonese, were almost all male and were generally twenty to thirty years old. The above description exactly fits the typical opium smoker in China at the time, so it's no surprise that the immigrant tide carried more than a few opium smokers to the kingdom.

The two groups traveled to their new homes by sea, but the circumstances were different and important. In California, the emigrants hoped to make their fortunes in the "Gold Mountains," as the United States, and especially California, was known. On arrival, they became miners or laborers or worked in businesses like laundries and restaurants or trades such as cigar making. Although the Chinese tended to cluster together, those going to America could live wherever they wanted (subject to the usual racial bias

Chinese contract laborers arriving at Honolulu to begin their five-year contracts. *Archives of Hawaii.*

and segregationist tendencies of the White majority at the time). Beginning in 1852, however, Hawaii brought the Chinese in as contract laborers. These sugar workers lived on plantations earning twenty-five cents per day six days per week for the five-year duration of their contracts.

Hawaii discovered it had an opium problem fairly quickly after the contract laborers started arriving. The sugar planters, having gone to some expense to bring the laborers to the islands, wanted them sober and fit for the six days each week they were paying for and objected to opium for business reasons. One observer at the time wrote, "Opium takes away a man's strength. He becomes a lazy fellow and will not work, and he cannot do the same work as a man who does not use opium."

These weren't the only reservations about the drug. The New England missionaries who had come to the islands decades before had objections to the practice on moral grounds, and these people wielded considerable influence on the islands' *ali`i*, or ruling class. Those ali`i already had bitter experience with alcohol and wanted to avoid the impact of another intoxicant on a Native Hawaiian population that was already shrinking at an alarming rate.

As early as 1856, the kingdom began trying to legislate its way around its opium problem, a pattern that the United States would follow thirty years later. The first effort was a measure that prohibited opium sales, except on a doctor's prescription. The law was filled with loopholes and had no mechanism for enforcement, so unsurprisingly, it failed. After attempting to tighten the statute in 1859, the government opted for a new and radically different approach.

In 1860, the legislature approved an act to "allow unrestricted sale of opium to Chinamen only." The law provided for three licenses that would be sold at auction, essentially creating a monopoly similar to the one operating in the British crown colony of Hong Kong, known informally as "the farm." For the next fourteen years, opium was imported, sold and consumed legally, a business that made several Chinese businessmen extremely wealthy as they supplied a growing population of opium smokers.

Hawaii's government benefited from the license fees, import duties and other taxes, but sales increased yearly, as did opium-related problems in Honolulu's Chinatown. Opponents of opium continued to press for the drug to be banned, and in 1874, their arguments prevailed, and the kingdom returned to prohibition. The open and regulated trade disappeared, replaced immediately by a black market supplied by smugglers who brought opium from Hong Kong, Victoria, British Columbia and San Francisco, where sales were still legal. Prices in Honolulu soared.

Many in Honolulu, including Chinese businessmen and government officials, had fond memories of the earlier period and made efforts over the next decade to bring it back. None of these were successful until the legislature of 1886 passed a licensing bill. This measure took effect on January 1, 1887, and was immediately controversial, with charges of corruption reaching the newspapers soon after. The new licensee, son of Hawaii's first Chinese millionaire Chun Afong, began importing the five tons of opium he needed to supply the five to seven thousand smokers in the islands. Prices dropped, and the black market, unable to compete with the legal and regulated one, dried up, and smuggling became unprofitable.

This situation didn't last. Fed by credible allegations that King David Kalakaua himself had accepted a large bribe to award the same license to two different individuals, his political opponents staged a bloodless coup, forcing the king to sign a new constitution that severely curbed his power. Now a reigning monarch rather than a ruling one, Kalakaua could not prevent a special session of the legislature from repealing the licensing law and returning the kingdom to prohibition at the end of 1887.

The change in opium's legal status had immediate and significant ramifications. The black market returned, and once again, opium prices in Honolulu climbed to as much as sixty dollars per pound, far more than the ten or twelve dollars in California. And the large number of smokers and their demand for five or six tons of opium each year meant the trade in Hawaii could be serviced only by a ring using its own ship. The timing was perfect for *Halcyon* and its crew. By 1890, William Whaley and Ewen McLean were on the way to the islands.

11

CLEARS FOR YOKOHAMA

On January 13, 1890, a low black schooner cast off from its mooring in Victoria's harbor, riding the outgoing tide toward the open ocean. *Halcyon*'s master, Alfred Metcalf, had filed papers with the custom house, declaring it to be bound for Yokohama "in ballast," or empty of any cargo. He and his crew had worked hard over the past few weeks to put out the word that they were headed out on a sealing expedition, going to try their luck in the islands off Japan. Nobody believed that, of course. Real sealers carried specialized equipment, canoes and small boats, rifles and experienced hunters. *Halcyon* had none of these, just a scratch crew of five and the same captain that had brought in seventeen sealskins one year "just for show."

Metcalf's crew was a mix of Canadians and Americans, everybody signed on for a voyage they knew could take as much as a year, but which they all hoped would end in a big payday. *Halcyon*'s mate for the trip was James Harvey, a veteran of Victoria's sealing fleet and an old hand in the North Pacific waters. Bill Johnson and Joseph Lippett joined as able seamen. Johnson was single and American. He and Harvey had crewed aboard *Halcyon* on some of the earlier voyages to California, spending the off times together and developing a friendship so close that people joked that they could be identified as "Me and Bill." Lippett, thirty-one, from Victoria, was the only married man in the crew, but he wouldn't be seeing his wife for almost a year and a half. The last man, essential to this venture, might have been a bit uneasy as the schooner rose to meet the first of the Pacific swells at the harbor's mouth. Constantine Capilos, ship's cook, came to the *Halcyon* from Demetrius Camarinos and George Lycurgus, Whaley's Greek partners and customers. Capilos, forty-one, a former waiter and chef in San Francisco restaurants, was a Greek immigrant from Sparta and naturalized American but was no sailor.

The customs men watched the *Halcyon* go and the man from the *Daily Colonist*, too. Every snitch, tout and stool pigeon on the waterfront passed the word to the American consul. That word would be on the next PCSS steamer going south and on the first Canada Mail ship headed for Hawaii and Japan; *Halcyon* had gone to sea.

It was mid-January in the North Pacific, definitely the worst time of the year to try a crossing from Victoria to Yokohama. Modern television viewers are familiar with the weather in these waters from shows such as *Deadliest Catch*, and the storms facing *Halcyon* and its crew were the same ones that shoot thirty- and forty-foot waves 2,000 miles south to crash onto Oahu's North Shore surfing beaches. *Halcyon* faced 4,474 miles of that in January, February and March. For much of the time the prevailing winds would be against the ship, and for the entire trip, it would be off the main shipping lanes, alone in a cold, dark sea. As the snow-covered mountains of Vancouver Island dropped below the horizon behind them, the men in the schooner got down to work.

Twenty-five hundred miles to the south and in much balmier climes, Will Whaley decided that he liked Honolulu—a lot. He'd arrived in the islands in October, staying through Christmas and spending some very pleasant hours in the company of Peter Camarinos and making friends with the Chinese businessmen who were so important for their mutual success. The party only got livelier when George Lycurgus came back into town in January aboard the SS *Australia*. Lycurgus, a poker buddy with none other than King David Kalākaua, introduced Whaley to all sorts of interesting people, and Will, who was supposed to leave town in early March, postponed his trip twice, reluctantly sailing for San Francisco on April 11 aboard the *Australia*.

Before he left, though, one of the opium ring's members said Lycurgus introduced Whaley to Hawaii's reigning monarch. The two smugglers joined some of the very convivial games held at the king's boathouse, Healani, in Honolulu Harbor. The King of the Opium Ring partied heartily with the King of Hawaii. It's a good story, and it might have the virtue of being true. We know that Whaley did meet Hawaiian royalty on his next trip to the islands.

Aboard SS *Australia*, a regular on the Honolulu–San Francisco run and Will Whaley's ride to the islands in 1889. *Bancroft Library, University of California, Berkeley.*

He was supposed to be taking care of business, but wherever he was, Will Whaley was always being Whaley, and it's difficult to believe that he would turn down an opportunity to drink, smoke, play cards and generally pal around with David Kalākaua, who liked to do all of those things too. Here's how one of his crewmen described the visit later: "He was put up at the club there and was always able to put up a swell front. He could talk with anyone, could Whaley. He wined and dined old King Kalākaua and was quite the thing in Hawaiian society."

When he wasn't partying, Whaley had real work to do in Honolulu, and it was critical to the operation's success. Before leaving town, he had to make arrangements to offload the cargo, finding a secluded spot where *Halcyon*'s crew could safely move the opium ashore. Whaley and a new friend lined up two ideal sites, both with easy access by the ring's Hawaii contacts and both at a safe distance from the Hawaiian customs service. Whaley wasn't too worried about them, anyway. The old customs officer had scoped out the opposing team and saw nothing but golden opportunity.

In San Francisco, Ewen McLean was looking at another kind of prospect as he packed for the long ocean voyage to Asia. This would be his first trip back to Hong Kong since he'd left there as a boy in 1876. Fourteen years later, he'd be returning as a successful businessman, the proprietor of a wholesale drug company. He'd also be returning as a family man. On May 5, he married Ella Julian, a twenty-three-year-old Californian from San Jose. The two young lovers tied the knot across the bay in Oakland.

Ella, who had been born Ella Macwee Wilson, was already a widow. She had married Charles Otis Julian when she was sixteen, and the couple produced a son, Charles Jr., who was seven when his mother went to the altar a second time. Young Charlie would be getting a brother or sister as part of the deal, as this was something of a shotgun wedding. Ella was four months pregnant, so Ewen was doing right by her, even if their honeymoon would be rather abbreviated. On May 8, only three days later, he boarded the SS *Gaelic* and sailed for Yokohama and Hong Kong.

Halcyon was already there. After a rough passage and enough high winds and seas to last the crew a lifetime, the schooner sailed up Tokyo Bay and anchored off Yokohama on April 28, a three-and-a-half-month adventure. While his crew went ashore to sample some of the port city's entertainment options, Metcalf reported at the American Consulate for Kanagawa Prefecture (Yokohama). He got a decidedly chillier reception than most American seamen expected when they reached Japan.

Consul-General Clarence R. Greathouse's main job was dealing with American captains and their American sailors. The consulate got a lot of complaints from seamen who had been shanghaied in San Francisco, Portland or Seattle and whose first port of call after that unpleasant experience was Yokohama. Some seamen wanted to file grievances against their captain or the mates on their ships, while others had pay issues or were annoyed about their treatment on the voyage. In many cases, Greathouse couldn't do much more than listen, but he meant to do something about Alfred Metcalf and his schooner yacht.

The consul had long since gotten word about *Halcyon*, its owners and its purpose for coming to Asia. Those dispatches on the Pacific Mail steamers made it clear that *Halcyon* had come for opium. Despite Metcalf's bland statements about the sealing grounds southeast of Japan, Greathouse fully expected him to head in a different direction when he left port. Greathouse had been a San Francisco lawyer and had relatives in the city, including one who had raced on the bay against the notorious schooner. He'd heard all of the smuggling stories and knew *Halcyon* by name and reputation. He took a personal interest and watched carefully as Metcalf did his business in town.

That business included "meeting with a Chinaman ashore." This man, Chun Kin, was someone that Greathouse already suspected of involvement in opium smuggling. Whatever the Chinese comprador was up to, he didn't have any interests in sealing, which further convinced the consul that Metcalf and his ship were up to no good. In a meeting with Metcalf, the captain told Greathouse that *Halcyon*'s owner, Alfred [*sic*] Wilson was expected in Yokohama any day. This was also unusual; unless he was also the ship's captain, the owners of the American and Canadian sealers did not normally travel with their ships. Sealing was an uncomfortable, unpleasant, dangerous and downright ugly business, one best left to the hired help.

Metcalf had other meetings in Yokohama. The *Gaelic*, with Ewen McLean aboard, arrived in town on May 23, staying long enough for McLean to meet with Whaley at the Grand Hotel and pay a call on his skipper before leaving again for Hong Kong. Metcalf told his principals about the surly attitude at the American consulate and that if they were harboring any illusions that *Halcyon*'s mission was still a big secret, they could forget those right now.

This called for a change in plan or at least another misdirection, and Whaley came up with one. As he and McLean headed south for Hong Kong, Metcalf put out the word that he was going in the same direction. *Halcyon* needed "special repairs" and fitting out that could only be obtained in Hong Kong. This meant taking a 3,600-mile round trip detour down to the crown colony. (This voyage, even if uneventful, practically guaranteed that *Halcyon* wouldn't be able to get back to the sealing grounds in the Bonins

The Grand Hotel, Yokohama's finest and the headquarters for the ring's Japan operations. *Postcard, author's collection.*

Hong Kong waterfront in 1890. This was the center of the world's opium trade when *Halcyon* arrived in July. *Wikipedia.*

before the weather closed in and the season ended, so it's no surprise that nobody believed the story.) Metcalf had the men spread this word in the bars and brothels, and he passed it to the skeptical Clarence Greathouse before *Halcyon* upped anchor and sailed down the bay at the beginning of July.

None of this fooled Greathouse. He sent dispatches off to Washington, saying that he was convinced *Halcyon* was going south to get opium at Hong Kong. He also took the opportunity to warn his fellow diplomatic representatives in town of *Halcyon*'s coming, saying, "I am satisfied that this schooner did not come to Yokohama on any legitimate business." He then notified the American diplomatic mission in Hong Kong. His message went to Consul-General Robert E. Withers, a former colonel in the Confederate army. Withers had inherited the job from another, much better-known Confederate, General John Singleton Mosby, the "Gray Ghost of the Confederacy," and the former rebels ran a tight ship in the consulate that covered both Hong Kong and the Portuguese colony of Macao, nearby. They were also just as hostile to American opium smugglers. Withers got the message and was waiting when *Halcyon* showed up on July 16, just as Greathouse had predicted, Metcalf checking in and giving the phony "we came for repairs" cover story.

Will Whaley and Ewen McLean were already settled in and waiting when their schooner arrived, all of them together at last in the opium capital of the world. *Halcyon* and the King of the Opium Ring had made it to the promised land.

12

ALL THE OPIUM IN THE WORLD

HONG KONG IN 1890

It had taken a little longer than anticipated, raised a few more eyebrows than they'd wanted and cost more than anyone expected, but Whaley's plan was back on track. If all went well in Hong Kong, they'd all be home in Victoria before the winter gales began.

First things first, they had opium to buy, which was a job for Will Whaley and his Chinese-speaking partner, Ewen McLean. They went looking for the best, figuring that they hadn't come all this way for anything less. The best in 1890 meant Lai Yuen, the preferred marque in Honolulu and San Francisco, and one of the few brands on the market good enough that counterfeiters copied the labels and the metal stamps on the tins. There should be no problem getting Lai Yuen; it was the premier product of the Hong Kong monopoly and had been for years. Except this year, there was a hitch. To understand the problem, we need a little background on the opium business as it was structured in Asia generally and Hong Kong in particular. This requires a brief history of the unsavory but lucrative trade that created Hong Kong in the first place.

Opium smoking didn't start in China; it was a foreign habit introduced by Dutch traders from the East Indies in the seventeenth century. The Chinese knew about opium, as they had used it in medicine and cultivated the opium poppy plant for centuries. When the smoking habit started to catch on in China, the government, which saw the ill effects on the smokers, didn't like it. The Chinese emperor and his government also resented the impact of opium on the country's trade balance, which up until then had been all weighted in China's favor. China sold tea and other goods to the Western merchants from the one port opened to the traders at Canton (now Guangzhou) but did not purchase much, if anything, from the disappointed foreigners who had to bring silver on the ships carrying cargo away from China.

Opium changed that equation, balancing the scale, and by the late 1830s, the Chinese were spending more on opium than the British and others were spending on tea. Plus, years of buying and smoking opium had created millions of addicts in southern China. This made the foreigners happy, but from the emperor on down, the Chinese were displeased. To rebalance the scale, the emperor sent an emissary to Canton with instructions to put a stop to the opium trade.

Commissioner Lin Tse-hsu (also written Lin Zexu) did a bang-up job, following the emperor's orders to the letter. Lin arrived in Guangdong Province in March 1839, arresting 1,700 local opium dealers and confiscating more than seventy thousand opium pipes. Then he went after the Western opium merchants, making them an offer for their opium that they couldn't refuse. The merchants refused anyway, but Lin had the power to literally starve the merchants in their factories in Canton, and he used it. The hungry traders caved fairly quickly, turning over 20,283 chests, 2.6 million pounds of opium, an entire year's crop. It took five hundred of Lin's men twenty-three days to destroy the haul, still the world's record drug bust.

The mostly British merchants didn't take kindly to the loss of their merchandise or to Lin's cheeky open letter to Queen Victoria, asking whether the ruler of the "barbarians" had any conscience about the evils of the opium trade, and they attacked the Chinese forces. This led to a three-year "opium war," which eventually resulted in an overwhelming British victory. The 1842 Treaty of Nanking, which settled the terms of the peace following the First Opium War, included three very important provisions. First, it legalized the opium trade in China. Second, it awarded the island of Hong Kong to the British, where it would be the center of the booming traffic for the next eighty years. Finally, the treaty opened other ports besides Canton to foreign trade, exposing even more of China to outside influence, including the opium business. It would take a few years and another opium war to complete the process, but the British turned that business into a machine that poured opium from India into China on an industrial scale. Large segments of the Chinese population, particularly in the southeast part of the country near Canton and Hong Kong, were addicted, keeping the traffic flowing at a rapid clip.

In Hong Kong itself, the opium traders established themselves in impressive buildings near the waterfront they and the Royal Navy now controlled. To handle the business in the new crown colony, the government elected to establish a licensed monopoly, awarding the license at an auction for a set period, usually one or two years. This monopoly, which became known as "the farm," was a source of enormous wealth and power to the farmer, and the license tended to shift back and forth between the same groups or syndicates over the years. At the same time, those license fees paid for a substantial part of the colonial government's budget. In 1890, the farm generated HK$477,600 of a total budget of HK$1,995,220 or 23.9 percent, an all-time high, so it was a system that made almost everybody happy. (The Chinese government in Peking—now Beijing—wasn't happy, and as this is written in 2021, they haven't forgotten the whole episode and still aren't happy about it.)

Since the British had more guns and better ones, they didn't care whether the Chinese were happy or not, and when Whaley and the boys arrived some years later, the whole opium business had settled into a comfortable and very profitable routine. Opium was cultivated in vast amounts in British India and transported in British ships to Hong Kong. Once it got there, it could move on in three different directions. By far the largest quantity was the massive tonnage headed for the internal Chinese market and its millions of users. A significant amount was refined by the farmer for local consumption. Finally, the last but very important *jinshan yangao*, or "Gold Mountain opium," was destined for consumption overseas. This was the opium in the famous Lai Yuen and Fook Lung brand tins sought after by consumers in California and in other overseas Chinese communities throughout the Pacific. Gold Mountain opium accounted for 60 to 75 percent of the raw opium refined by the monopoly in Hong Kong, the remainder being consumed locally by Hong Kong's thirty-five thousand addicts. The farm had things very well organized and thoroughly structured, with the profits flowing to the (Chinese) license holder and the (British) colonial government.

In 1882, two former rivals for the farm license, the Yan Wo and Wo Hang groups merged, bidding successfully for the farm and holding it for the next four years under the name of the Sing Wo Company, the parent company of Sing Wo Chan in Victoria. In 1886, however, Sing Wo got a rude surprise when a Singapore group, the Fook Tuck Company, won the concession with a higher bid. Fook Tuck now had the monopoly in Hong Kong, to be sure, but the Sing Wo Company still had an ace in the hole—it owned the brand names Lai Yuen and Fook Lung, the two most popular in the Hong Kong

Lai Yuen brand opium tin, five-taels. Imported at San Francisco in October 1898 aboard SS *Hong Kong Maru*. *Author's collection.*

and export trades. Everyone in Victoria, San Francisco, Honolulu and even Hong Kong wanted those two brands. After 1887, Sing Wo couldn't provide them from Hong Kong any longer, but the game was still afoot. They would just have to play it thirty-seven miles away across the water in another colonial outpost. Sing Wo and all its customers were going to Macao.

Like Hong Kong, Macao operated a licensed opium monopoly, and the Portuguese quickly turned their "farm" over to a new farmer, the Sing Wo Company, formerly of Hong Kong. Sing Wo didn't even change the labels on its Lai Yuen and Fook Lung tins, some still showing the "Hong Kong" point of origin. In fact, the Macao farm would continue to operate long after the Hong Kong monopoly went out of business, its opium eventually becoming more sought after than the counterpart across the water.

It posed a problem in 1890, though, for an opium smuggler who came to Hong Kong looking to buy Lai Yuen. Will Whaley and Ewen McLean hoped to fill their schooner with tins of Hong Kong's number one opium export, only to find that the local monopoly didn't carry that trademark anymore. The Hong Kong farmer helpfully offered them some other jinshan yangao brands, but Whaley declined; he had a ship, and Macao was only another half-day's sailing away. They'd come this far; they might as well go the distance to get what they'd come for.

The flamboyant smuggler was having a fine time in Hong Kong, where he lived "like a prince" and "continued to spend money like water." Whaley "had himself photographed in his Chinese toggery in company with two rich Chinese, who shared his revels," commissioned a painting of *Halcyon* under sail in Hong Kong harbor and held lavish and extravagant parties aboard his yacht.

In between parties and while Whaley and McLean went down to Macao to make arrangements for the Lai Yuen, Metcalf made a show of getting the overhaul he'd supposedly detoured south to obtain. At the American consulate, Consul-General Withers kept an eye on his American compatriots, noting that *Halcyon*'s repairs did not seem to warrant the

Whaley and *Halcyon* offloading opium in Hawaii. A newspaper artist's impression of *Halcyon*'s 1891 voyage to Hawaii and the landing of opium on the Island of Lanai. Honolulu Star Bulletin.

three-thousand-mile diversion it'd made to get them. Everyone assumed *Halcyon* and its crew were in town for the usual reason, and nobody got too excited about it, since the "usual reason" pretty much accounted for Hong Kong's very existence.

Down in Macao, McLean and Whaley met with Macao opium farmers, arranging to purchase at a very good price 6,200 pounds of prime quality Hong Kong No. 1 (Lai Yuen) opium. The drug was packaged in the usual five-tael tins in sixty-two one-hundred-pound crates. These fit easily in *Halcyon*'s cabin, and McLean and Whaley headed back to Hong Kong with the deal closed and the money, paid in American silver trade dollars, the standard currency in use at the time. At the going rate for opium in Macao at around $3 per pound, or $18,600 for the load, they spent half of their working capital.

July turned to August, and the visit to Hong Kong wrapped up. Metcalf made ready for sea and took care of an important legal point as *Halcyon* prepared to cast off from its mooring in Hong Kong's harbor. The all-important ship's papers showed that it would be clearing Hong Kong in ballast. Metcalf and his crew were officially still sticking to the bogus sealing story, even though the season was nearing an end as the seas near Japan would turn cold and gray with autumn and winter approaching by the time *Halcyon* could arrive. In reality, Whaley and McLean had made other arrangements. Metcalf and the schooner would meet with a junk from Macao with the opium aboard, transferring the cargo at sea. This didn't fool

Consul-General Withers, who thought the whole idea that *Halcyon* had come and gone empty-handed was absurd.

Unaware that the authorities were on to their secret plan, or at least not caring, with their mission accomplished and their schooner safely on its way, Will Whaley and Ewen McLean relaxed for a few more days in Hong Kong before catching steamers back toward the United States. They looked forward to a substantial killing. Expecting profits approaching forty dollars per pound in Hawaii, they stood to make out like pirates on this deal *if* Metcalf could get *Halcyon* to the islands safely. On August 6, the schooner cleared Hong Kong, ostensibly bound for Victoria by way of the Bonin Islands, a hard sail ahead of it. Alfred Metcalf and his crew had no idea just how hard it was going to be.

13
SHIPWRECK!

THE END OF *HALCYON*?

In the end, there was nothing that Alfred Metcalf could have done that would have saved the ship. This was no ordinary storm, not even a typical August typhoon. This one would flood much of Japan, wreck railway lines, flatten villages and leave thousands homeless. The massive, implacable winds would also catch a small schooner and hurl it onto an unforgiving, rocky peninsula.

August was usually a good month to be crossing the North Pacific from west to east in a sailing vessel. The winds are usually fair, and the seas are as calm as they will ever be throughout the year. The men of the *Halcyon* had probably planned it this way, or maybe they were running a little late. Alfred Metcalf was hoping in any case to get across before the weather turned surly in October and November. In this August, Metcalf was tracking the Pacific Mail shipping routes, jogging north toward Yokohama and following the great circle that would carry his schooner and its cargo on a safe arc above the Mariana, Marshall and Gilbert Islands, all the way to Hawaii. As August waned, *Halcyon* hummed along, making beautiful headway, one lovely day passing into the next. The schooner's crew could be forgiven if they forgot one important point about August in the Western Pacific, something all the captains on the Yokohama and Hong Kong routes knew by heart. August is the middle of the typhoon season.

A storm came up on August 20—not a bad one, just heavy weather bringing high winds as the schooner reached Japan's southern islands. The winds and seas were favorable, and they crowded on more sail, running off

THE SCHOONER BLOSSOMED A SNOWY FLIGHT OF CANVAS AND CUT AND RAN FOR IT.

Halcyon at sea. A newspaper artist's impression of the infamous smuggler chased by a revenue cutter. San Francisco Examiner.

322 miles in a twenty-one-hour period, over 15.6 knots sustained, or 18 miles per hour. *Halcyon* sailed out of the storm into the sunshine, slowing to its more normal, though still rollicking, pace, but Metcalf was concerned. Keeping an eye on the eastern horizon, he told Harvey to secure the ship, and he altered his course to get clear of the dark bulk of Japan off his port side. Soon enough, the whole crew was watching as the clouds piled higher in the southeast and the winds began to rise again. Even cook Capilos knew they were in for a hard ride, and he put out the fire in the galley and secured all the locker doors.

Typhoons didn't have names in 1890, and mariners had no satellite images or early warning of their coming. This one rushed on *Halcyon* from the southeast, tracking westward across Honshu and then north along the west coast of the island of Hokkaido, creating a path of destruction, floods and wind damage. It took weeks to tote up the cost and months for the nation to recover. The typhoon caught *Halcyon* on its lower right quadrant, the fierce winds pushing the schooner toward the coast of Japan, where Metcalf definitely did *not* want to go. This was called a "lee shore," and sailors dreaded it. In the age of sail, ships went where the wind carried them. If something went wrong, if they lost a mast or sails blew out due to high winds or even if the crew just took in all the canvas and went "under bare poles," the ship could still drift safely, even fairly comfortably, at sea. But that only worked if there was no land downwind, no lee shore waiting to tear a sailing ship to pieces, because if there was, almost nothing a captain or crew did could stop it happening.

It was happening to Metcalf, and he knew it. Night had closed in, and the clouds, miles thick and full of driving rain, cut visibility to near zero. He had a rough idea where he was, somewhere near the entrance to Tokyo Bay. The pressing question was how far north? If he was too far, he risked hitting the rocky Boso Peninsula, the unforgiving promontory that guards the bay's east side. If he was south of the peninsula, he had an extra twenty miles of sea room to leeward, space to drift downwind before encountering the coast of Honshu Island. And if he'd gotten it just right, he might make the entrance to the bay and get into the Uraga Channel or one of the coves on either side, where he could find shelter from the wind and waves.

He had one last option, his anchors, and Metcalf would have known they weren't going to do him any good in this storm. The water was too deep, the waves too big and the winds too high. He put them out anyway, and they felt them catch and drag when they got closer to shore. By that time, they could see the surf in the darkness, the waves slamming into the rocks, spray bursting masthead height into the air. *Halcyon* drifted inexorably down toward the beach, and the whole crew gathered in the cockpit aft, getting ready to go into the cold, dark water.

Sometime after midnight on August 23, 1890, *Halcyon* drove ashore near Sunosaki at the foot of the Boso Peninsula in Chiba Prefecture. Alfred Metcalf missed the entrance to Tokyo Bay and shelter from the storm by a couple of miles at the most. The wreck was total, a storm surge and massive waves lifting the schooner over the shallows toward the beach, carrying it between deadly rocks, the surf exploding around them. When it crashed ashore, *Halcyon* became another fixed object for the waves' fury, and they pounded the ship relentlessly, filling the air with driving spray. The five men in the crew huddled in the open cockpit by the wheel; no one wanted to stay below and take the chance of being trapped inside a wrecked ship. Now they clung together, exposed to the worst the storm could throw at them, waiting for the end.

Constantine Capilos panicked first, leaping into the surf between waves, where he was knocked down and got back up, disappearing beneath a wall of water before emerging to pull himself up on the shingle, out of reach of the next wave. In the cockpit, now tilted at almost ninety degrees, the four remaining weighed their chances as the surf blasted them. *Halcyon* lay on its side, each successive wave knocking it back and forth across the beach, filling the cockpit where the men clutched the rails to keep from being swept into the darkness.

Harvey and Johnson, clinging to their "Me and Bill" bond, shouted at each other about trying for shore, looking to Metcalf with pale, wet, scared faces, the captain's nightmare dream come true. But Metcalf hesitated before giving the order to abandon ship. The wind still howled, and the waves still crashed over them, but it seemed to the master mariner that they weren't being thrown about quite so badly and the water wasn't reaching quite so high as before. He and the others looked out into the blackness and back at each other and started to hope.

A few hours later, with dawn breaking, all four of them stepped down out of the cockpit onto the black sand of the beach. Gray clouds full of rain still raced past high overhead, and the waves still pounded the rocks offshore, but where they stood qualified as dry land. In Alfred Metcalf's opinion, this called for a drink—maybe a couple of them. *Halcyon* looked to be a total loss, but the cargo was safe and so was the crew, so the disaster hadn't been complete. This was definitely cause for some celebration, and the crew joined the captain in a couple more drinks.

And as it turned out, some celebration was in order after all. Modeler W.G. Hall and builder William Stone had done their jobs well on Harry Tevis's schooner yacht. Metcalf and Harvey, along with a crowd of interested Japanese spectators from nearby Sunosaki, checked it out in the daylight and found, to their amazement, that after all the beating it had taken, *Halcyon*, though lying on its side, was basically sound. It wasn't so much wrecked as stranded, and the two men looked across the beach, the rocks, the line of surf and the ocean beyond. If they could get it back in the water, they might not be done yet. This called for another drink.

Word of wreck got out quickly. Messengers notified Tokyo, as the telegraph lines were down, and advised the Americans at Kanagawa, where *Halcyon*'s name was already mud. Consul George Scidmore, who had taken over when Clarence Greathouse was transferred to Korea, told the Japanese that he expected the schooner had opium aboard and to check it carefully. The Japanese Customs authorities were already on the way. Metcalf had his cover story ready, and the crew was in line. Since there was no hiding the fact that they had three tons of opium aboard, they needed an explanation for the customs men when they arrived. Metcalf provided it. The opium had been purchased in Macao and was being shipped to Victoria, British Columbia. Did he have papers proving that? He used to, but during the wreck, a wave had swept through the cabin and unfortunately carried the ship's papers out to sea.

It was an unlikely story, incredible even, but it couldn't be easily disproven. Metcalf, claiming illness, checked himself into a hospital in Yokohama and was unavailable for further interviews. The other crewmen swore ignorance, saying they'd signed on for a Victoria to Hong Kong to Victoria voyage. The Japanese suggested that maybe the *Halcyon*'s owners could obtain duplicate papers from Hong Kong. American consul Scidmore, who believed that Metcalf and his men were lying through their teeth and "up to no good," wanted more drastic action taken.

America and Japan had an 1860 treaty on this subject, he pointed out. The treaty prohibited Japanese people from landing opium in the United States and Americans from landing opium in Japan. Metcalf, an American, had done just that, even if he couldn't help himself, thanks to the typhoon, and Scidmore wanted the treaty enforced and the opium confiscated. It was very unusual for the American side to take a position against its citizen's interest, and as the Japanese pondered this oddity, a new player bounded onto the stage. William A. Whaley had come to Yokohama to save the day. Four days after the wreck, on August 27, Whaley arrived in Yokohama from the south. He'd sailed from Hong Kong on the 22nd on the SS *City of Rio de Janeiro*, booked through to San Francisco, but now he had work to do in Japan.

Getting the opium back from the Japanese was the main task, but Whaley wasn't stopping there. He looked over *Halcyon* sitting forlornly on the beach and then had a word with mate Jim Harvey and Bill Johnson, who were camped out at the wreck site, keeping any would-be looters away. Whaley came away with the firm conclusion that *Halcyon* might be high and dry now, but its smuggling days weren't over yet.

Leaving "Me and Bill" at the wreck site, he put Lippett and Capilos in a hotel in Yokohama while he fished around for some help, getting it from the Yokohama Engine and Iron Works Company, which agreed to help with the salvage effort for $1,750. They were on the job the next day, building a cradle under Jim Harvey's supervision. Alfred Metcalf was staying in the hospital for the time being "too sick" to talk to the authorities or anyone else. Whaley met with the Japanese customs officials who now had his 6,200 pounds of opium in their custody. Whaley stuck to Metcalf's story, claiming that the opium had been bound for Victoria to be sold there. He said he could prove this by getting duplicate papers from the shipper in Macao. In the meantime, the opium, which was never intended to be brought to Japan, should be placed in a bonded warehouse, and he would put up a cash bond to ensure that it would not be officially landed in the country.

Naturally, this proposal, which was a lie from beginning to end, outraged the American consul. Whaley met with him on September 1 and discovered that George Scidmore was every bit as dead certain as Greathouse had been that *Halcyon*'s cargo was headed for San Francisco's Chinatown, or Seattle's or Portland's. He was just as unfriendly to Whaley and told him and everybody else who would listen that he and the United States government wanted the dope taken and destroyed. *Halcyon*, an American ship with a mostly American crew, had broken Japanese law and violated a treaty and by God, Scidmore wanted something done about it! The Japanese, who had the opium, took Whaley's money, said they'd think about it and suggested he see about those duplicate ship's papers. Since it didn't look like *Halcyon* was going anywhere anytime soon, this seemed like a reasonable position to everybody except Scidmore.

Whaley caught a steamer south for Hong Kong, leaving Harvey in charge of things at Sunosaki. With the help of the salvage company, they managed to raise the seventy-five-ton schooner upright and get it into the cradle. Next, they unshipped all of the ballast that they could reach, lightening the schooner considerably. Then, they started hauling the whole contraption across country. Because of the rocks and shoals offshore, they couldn't put it into the water where it lay, so they mapped out a route overland to Tateyama Bay, about five miles away as the crow flies and quite a bit farther by the path they carved out, and began dragging *Halcyon* back home.

For this plan to work, they needed labor, and they had plenty of that nearby. *Halcyon* had come to rest almost exactly on the border between two villages, and the people from both of them were happy to get the paying jobs that came with being on the draglines in front of *Halcyon* and its cradle. Harvey discovered that he had more than enough manpower, which quickly turned into a bad thing as the competition to work on the schooner's salvage pitted the villagers against each other. If Harvey chose one village, those from the other made trouble, blocking the path and looting *Halcyon* when they got the chance. Harvey tried switching off, dividing the work so each village got a fair share. This Solomon-like attempt ended up annoying everyone, and the looting continued until the schooner had been "stripped bare."

It took more than three months to drag *Halcyon* from its resting place on the beach to the calm water of Tateyama Bay. Some days they made only a few yards, Harvey and Johnson camping out next to the yacht every night and working with the salvage team every day. They made minor repairs on the way and major ones when they reached Tateyama, where there were some facilities and a sheltered anchorage. In December, with Metcalf finally back from the hospital and Whaley returned from Hong Kong, they put *Halcyon* in the water. Whaley had been very upset about the looting, raising a major fuss with the Japanese authorities, who sent police officers down to guard *Halcyon* during the last legs of the strange road trip. Whaley didn't leave it there, getting a lawyer and making big noise about suing for the damages.

This was another smart play on Whaley's part. He'd come back from Hong Kong and Macao with papers that backed up his story 100 percent, of course. He knew, as everyone did, that you could buy just about anything you needed in Hong Kong, including ship's papers that would say whatever you wanted them to say. He also came back with another edge. All of that looting, particularly the latest, which had occurred under the supposedly watchful eyes of the Japanese police officers sent to stop it, caused a major loss of face for the customs officials and others who were preparing to make a ruling about Whaley's opium. Now, he and his attorney were threatening to sue the villagers, the police *and* the government for its negligence, a nasty, embarrassing and public flogging that those officials didn't relish. Much better to send *Halcyon* and its opium on their way as quickly and quietly as possible.

This solution left George Scidmore at the American consulate in what passes in the diplomatic world as a flaming rage, but as it turned out, his anger was premature. Winter wasn't yet over, and neither were those winter storms off the coast of Japan. Nature might yet do what the law and diplomacy could not. One of those storms brewed on February 11—not a typhoon but a strong enough southerly gale, driving up northward into Tokyo Bay and slamming sideways into normally placid Tateyama. Incredibly, Alfred Metcalf wasn't prepared for this storm either, which threw *Halcyon* ashore once more.

The latest wreck was more of a grounding; a tugboat easily pulled it off the beach, but there was more damage to contend with and new repairs to be made. Patience with Alfred Metcalf must have been wearing rather thin; two shipwrecks in one voyage are two more than the standard allotment for sea captains. A frustrated Will Whaley, still hanging about in Yokohama but anxious to get the long-stalled plan underway, hurried the supplies aboard and saw to the repairs personally. Metcalf's authority (and probably quite a bit of his master mariner's credibility) had withered away. Whaley had him bring *Halcyon* up the bay to Yokohama for the final refitting, getting the whole crew back from the brothels and adult entertainment facilities of Yokohama and ready to sail.

By the end of February, the day had finally come, and Whaley watched as *Halcyon* swept down the bay toward the open sea. At the consulate, Scidmore sent dispatches to San Francisco, alerting the authorities there that the schooner had left with at least three tons of opium aboard. The Pacific Mail ships and others on the transpacific route would carry the word to Honolulu and Victoria, too, arriving long before *Halcyon*. Whaley himself boarded the NYK Line steamship SS *Yamashiro Maru* on February 27, bound for Honolulu and San Francisco. The steam powered ship would get him to Hawaii two weeks before *Halcyon* even entered the neighborhood. But in San Francisco, word of *Halcyon*'s departure arrived weeks too late to save the life of one of the members of the ring and the job of another. Back in San Francisco, the opium game had gotten bloody.

14

COOKED BOOKS, SHATTERED DREAMS AND SUDDEN DEATH

At the rail of the SS *Umatilla*, the sailor with the evening watch stood with the night inspector and watched the lady climb into the waiting hack onto Broadway Wharf. They'd seen her come to the gangway with *Umatilla*'s purser, observed the farewell kiss and commented on her obvious attractions. That purser was a lucky man, they agreed, as the cab moved slowly down the wharf, and the sound of a gunshot, muted by the fog, echoed in the darkness.

It was 11:00 p.m. on January 25, 1891, and the men who rushed to the cabin of purser Frank J. Curtin found a terrible sight. A bullet had pierced the young man's head and a revolver lay on the floor next to his body. Curtin was still breathing, but anyone could see that he wasn't long for this world. The bullet fired through his left temple had exited the right and shattered a mirror on the wall. The watch called *Umatilla*'s captain and the police, but it was obvious that this was a suicide. The cops wanted to know why a popular, well-liked and respected ship's officer would take so desperate a step, and such a final one. The captain, who had overseen Curtin's work on the *Umatilla*, said Mr. George Perkins, a director of the shipping line, had spoken to the young man only the day before about the two issues that were every purser's bugbear—drink and a possible shortage in the accounts. Curtin admitted to a problem with the first, and a quick review of the books found a $1,500 shortfall.

Neither Perkins nor the captain knew about Curtin's secret, a "sure-thing" investment that had turned out to be anything but. And they didn't know

SS *Umatilla*. A regular on the San Francisco–Victoria-Skagway run, purser Frank Curtin served aboard until his suicide in January 1891. *1914 Post Card.*

that earlier on January 25, Curtin had spent the evening drinking with a friend who had the same problem. Both men were members of an opium ring, and they had been waiting a long, long time for their ship to come in. In January 1891, the schooner *Halcyon* was at least three months overdue, and word had reached San Francisco from Japan that there was a good chance it might not be coming back at all. For the men who had put up $40,000 in cash to finance what was supposed to be a nine-month smuggling run, the impact of this news ran the gamut from inconvenient to catastrophic.

Some of the investors were old hands at the business. Albert Weinrich Wilson anted up from Victoria, where he was keeping house. The little German with the bad cough had made a bundle on those runs down the coast, and he plowed some of that money back into this scheme when Whaley and McLean proposed it. So did C.S. Joslyn, who piled in with $6,000, enough to buy a ton and a half of Lai Yuen No. 1 at the pier in Macao. The wharf rat, A.J. Smith, also quite successful from previous smuggling runs, eagerly anted up on this one. Smith, whose freight clerk job at the Broadway Wharf allowed him to help out some of those ad hoc smugglers, had been making money on the side steadily over the years. He'd made a couple of legitimate investments with the proceeds of earlier *Halcyon* wins, buying a tugboat and some ranch land outside San Francisco. With a big killing in sight, Smith was all in.

Three new investors joined the party. German confectioner George Wichman ran a candy store downtown with his brother and had enough money left over to throw in with the smugglers. Wichman didn't have any criminal background or experience in the smuggling game. He followed everyone else's lead on this scheme and waited for the money to roll in. His friend, a photographer's assistant named George N. Thomas, also thought he saw a pot of gold at the end of the *Halcyon* rainbow. Thomas, described as a "gentleman from a good family," was one of the most passive of the investors, letting his friend Wichman and the others do most of the talking as the months ticked by.

Louis Greenwald, a sometime bookkeeper, clerk, professional gambler and general layabout, rounded out the investment side. Personality-wise, Greenwald was the exact opposite of Thomas, taking an active role in monitoring the operation's progress and bugging McLean about the status of his investment. Greenwald was officially unemployed and involved in a couple of shady schemes. He was getting married shortly but lived in town with his brother, Moses, both of them California natives from Humboldt County, up north. Greenwald, with a wine stain birthmark under his right eye, was a distinctive character. He'd grown up in Arcata, California, two years behind Will Whaley at Union High School. The boys lived a block apart in their school years, reconnecting when they became smuggling conspirators together in 1888.

For these investors, *Halcyon*'s voyage was an opportunity to make a major score, but first, their ship quite literally had to come in, and there were a lot of things that could go wrong on a venture like this. Nature could wreck the best laid plans at any point along the fourteen-thousand-mile round trip. Pirates still prowled the waters off the Philippines and along the Chinese coast, looking to snatch up small, unwary ships. The customs men in Hawaii, ordinarily an inept lot, might get lucky, as they did on occasion, a bribed inspector could fall ill on the appointed day or worse have an attack of conscience. Anything could happen, and in August 1890, a typhoon had. Making things right again took too long for Frank Curtin, who knew his books couldn't stand the kind of look that would disgrace him and his family. *Halcyon* might still come in, but it would be too late for the young man from Victoria, who shot himself before the schooner ever left Japan.

Things weren't much better for A.J. Smith. The freight clerk at Broadway Wharf had books, too, and he'd been cooking them in anticipation of a *Halcyon* payday. When that was delayed again and again, Smith finally got caught out, either through his association with Curtin or through some other lead. Goodall, Nelson fired him and threatened prosecution. Smith made up the shortage by selling his ranch land and tugboat, assets he'd bought with the money from previous scores. This kept the police out of the case, but

Left: Louis Greenwald. A gambler and investor in *Halcyon*'s Hawaii run, Greenwald was a boyhood friend and neighbor of Will Whaley in Arcata. *San Quentin prison records, California State Library, Sacramento.*

Below: SS *Umatilla* leaving from Broadway Wharf in San Francisco for the Klondike in 1914. *University of Alaska–Fairbanks*

the pressure on the ring's members was building. They needed some good news, and finally, they got some. In San Francisco, the SS *Gaelic* brought word at the beginning of April that at least $150,000 worth of opium was coming, and customs collector Timothy Phelps in said he'd send the revenue cutters out for a look. Phelps and everyone else on the West Coast would be disappointed. Metcalf and *Halcyon* and Will Whaley were all headed for Queen Lili'uokalani's Hawaii.

15

WITH EVERY HAND AGAINST HER

HALCYON RETURNS

The Pacific is the world's largest ocean by far, and as February ended and March began, *Halcyon* disappeared into it, an eighty-three-foot speck in sixty-three million square miles of water. The customs men in the United States and Hawaii knew the ship was coming, of course. As fleet as it was, the big Pacific Mail steamers leaving Yokohama like clockwork would put into port weeks before *Halcyon*, a sailing vessel and always at the mercy of the wind, could make it to its destination. The secret of that destination was the ship's second advantage—no one outside the ring knew exactly where the schooner was bound, which left hundreds if not thousands of miles of coastline to watch.

Those watching and waiting for *Halcyon* were uncomfortably aware that all those miles of coastline were mostly unguarded. The American Revenue Cutter Service had four cutters on the West Coast, but the *Bear*, *Corwin* and *Rush* generally laid up during the winter months and patrolled Alaskan waters during the warmer sealing season, and the *Wolcott* worked on Puget Sound. Collector of customs Timothy Phelps in San Francisco, knowing of *Halcyon*'s coming, announced his intention to send the cutters out after it, which failed to impress the newsmen covering the story. The collectors in Washington and Oregon were on the alert, too. In Hawaii, which had no revenue cutters at all, the Customs Service would charter a small steamer, arming it with a couple of Gatling guns and some artillery pieces in case it managed to chug up alongside *Halcyon* in a dead calm. In San Diego, a band of vigilantes, probably drunk, announced that they were going out after *Halcyon* to try and take it on the high seas for the reward money, and *they* went to sea, heavily armed and dangerous on what legally amounted to a pirating expedition. Everyone else sat back and waited for the leading lady to make an appearance.

Archibald S. Cleghorn. Hawaii's collector general of customs in 1891. *Archives of Hawaii.*

Halcyon made its star turn on March 31, when the crew of the Hawaiian coaster *Ka Moi* sighted a black schooner off the coast of Lanai Island. The *Ka Moi* turned to close with the stranger, which put on sail and sprinted off, disappearing into the distance. Another sighting followed on April 14, near the Island of Oahu. Two weeks later, Captain Kaai of the schooner *Haleakala*, a fair flyer, encountered the same ship off Lanai again, near the fearsome sea cliffs called the Pali Kaholo, a point normally avoided by sensible mariners. When Kaai made to approach, the dark schooner "pulled away like a racing yacht" and was soon out of sight.

The two reports of sightings off Lanai jolted the normally somnolent Hawaiian customs men into action. Collector General Archibald S. Cleghorn, a Scotsman who had married into a prominent Hawaiian family and produced a daughter, the beautiful Princess Kaiulani, heir to Hawaii's throne, had a difficult job ahead of him. Cleghorn supervised a staff of about thirty, most of whom worked in Honolulu. He had nobody at all on Lanai, a small, pork chop–shaped island about seventy-five miles from Honolulu.

Uninhabited except for some cowboys and a few farmers, Lanai was a fine place for offloading contraband in private. It had two remote beaches where small boats could land, no real harbors with a lot of other ships coming and going and, best of all, no police or customs men whatsoever. On the rare occasions when the handful of islanders needed law enforcement, a sheriff's deputy would be sent over from Lahaina, Maui, about eight miles away across the water. The sheriff's deputy knew all the people on the island and knew the territory intimately, far better than anyone Cleghorn would be able to send down from Honolulu. For a few years, that deputy had been Thomas E. Evans, a Welsh Canadian who had also married a socially prominent Hawaiian woman, which landed him a couple of civil service jobs, including postmaster in Lahaina and superintendent of the Hansen's

Royalty visits an opium smuggler. Hawaii's King David Kalākaua (*standing at center*) visits the Lahaina home of Thomas E. Evans (*standing, third left*), then deputy sheriff for Lahaina and Lanai, with French Prince Henri de Bourbon (*seated in carriage*). *Archives of Hawaii.*

Disease (leprosy) colony at Kalaupapa on the nearby island of Molokai. Now no longer a sheriff's deputy, Tommy Evans divided his time between Maui and Honolulu, where he'd become quite chummy with a visiting Californian named Will Whaley.

From Whaley's point of view, Lanai was almost a perfect spot for the smugglers of the opium ring. It was far enough from Honolulu to be away from police and customs interference but close enough to Maui that smaller boats could easily get there to collect the cargo. The shipping lanes all ran north and east of the island. *Halcyon* could loiter off the west coast, especially behind the steep sea cliffs of the Pali Kaholo, for days or even weeks without seeing another sail. Manele Bay and Hulupo`e Bay, the two coves where a boat could approach to land cargo, were right at the southeast end of the island. Today, a world class resort and golf course overlook these white sand beaches where tourists sun themselves. In 1891, a dark schooner dropped anchor just offshore and sent a boat in to the placid beach at Manele Bay with crates full of small tin boxes, and no one outside the opium ring was any the wiser.

In Honolulu, Cleghorn took stock of the situation. It hadn't really improved, even with the firmer evidence of *Halcyon*'s presence in Hawaiian waters. The schooner could outrun anything he could put to sea to chase it, and the warnings from his American counterparts and the informers in Victoria and San Francisco were alarming, even if most of them were probably false. One story held that the eighty-three-foot schooner was bringing 450 tons of opium, an absurdly inflated amount, but the most disquieting rumor was that Whaley had armed *Halcyon* with several cannon and that the crew was trained and ready to use them. American revenue cutters might be able to confront such a threat, but the Hawaiians had nothing to match it. And Cleghorn suspected it didn't matter. If the reports were correct, *Halcyon* had already been hovering offshore for two or three weeks, plenty of time to get its cargo ashore. The opium likely was on its way to Chinatown right now, and only a few days after *Haleakala*'s brief chase of *Halcyon*, Cleghorn got some hard evidence that Will Whaley's ship had finally come in.

In Honolulu, William Sheldon, one of Cleghorn's officers, had been carrying on something of a one-man crusade against opium smugglers for a couple of years. Sheldon made quite a few seizures, mostly small but a few big ones here and there. He wasn't doing all this work entirely out of spite; it was more likely that he and his informers were in it for the reward money they made from the sale of the seized opium and the 50 percent of any fines collected from the convicted smuggler.

Whatever his motives, on April 20, 1891, Sheldon got very suspicious of three trunks that came off an interisland steamship, the SS *Mokolii*, just arrived from Molokai and Lanai. The trunks, which seemed to be of Chinese manufacture, were marked "Glass, Handle With Care" and "were of strange weight," and Sheldon resolved to hold them long enough to see who came to pick them up. It proved to be a teamster, who carried the trunks a week later to a rented house near the beach in Waikiki, where Sheldon and two police officers were waiting. They pounced, finding 280 tins of Lai Yuen opium and a flustered Thomas E. Evans, who had just come over himself on the *Mokolii* from Lahaina and Lanai before that.

Sheldon and the police arrested Evans. Local businessman John Phillips floated Evans's $1,000 bail and got him an attorney for his trial, scheduled for May, as Cleghorn finally moved to intercept *Halcyon* before it could escape or more opium could be landed. The day after Evans's arrest, the customs chief and queen's marshal Charles Wilson chartered the interisland steamer *Claudine*, the fastest ship available, which wasn't saying a lot. He found some royal guardsmen, police and customs officers to man the steamer, mounted a couple of Gatling guns and a pair of small artillery pieces borrowed from the guard and dispatched the impromptu revenue cutter, with Wilson aboard, toward Lanai.

A substantial number of people in Honolulu were convinced that the "outgunned" *Claudine* had just departed on a suicide mission and were hoping it did not encounter *Halcyon*. These fears seemed to be confirmed when the roll of naval gunfire was reported off Lanai. Lurid tales of a sea battle came back to Honolulu, along with the grim word of the absent steamer's loss with all hands. Meanwhile, *Halcyon* had been sighted again, this time nearer to Honolulu, first off Oahu's southeast shore, then the northeast coast and finally hovering off the west side of the island at Waianae. That last report made sense to some in the custom house, as members of the opium ring, notably George Lycurgus and Demetrius Camarinos, were known to have leased property in the area. With no way to contact the missing *Claudine*, last heard from seventy-five miles away and watching the wrong island, a worried Cleghorn could only sit and wait.

More opium was showing up. In Hana, on Maui, Charlie Gray, a clerk on the interisland steamer *Kinau*, got into an argument on the street, knocking his adversary, a local judge, unconscious with the valise Gray was carrying. Unfortunately for Gray, the mighty blow broke open the valise, spilling fourteen tins of Lai Yuen opium onto the road. Like Evans, Gray had just arrived in town from Molokai and Lahaina, the trail seeming to point back the island of Lanai, just across the channel from Lahaina. Although he was arrested for the assault, Gray made bail and jumped it, catching an outbound sailing vessel for San Francisco. Back in Honolulu, the police arrested several Chinese gentlemen for possession of Lai Yuen, and a White woman named Campbell was relieved of several tins she had "concealed under her clothing."

The street price of opium dropped—a sure sign that the laws of supply and demand were working for Lai Yuen. Sheldon had been lucky but not lucky enough. Those three trunks that he'd seized were part of a larger shipment of twelve that were loaded aboard the *Mokolii* on Lanai. The other nine were missing, already gone to unknown receivers in Honolulu. Cleghorn suspected that one thousand pounds, and maybe double that, had already gotten past his men.

In fact, Cleghorn's chances of stopping the opium at the ports had dwindled to near zero, and they'd been close to that to begin with. His Customs Service was pathetically ill-equipped to handle a challenge like Whaley and the opium ring. Cleghorn had only a man or two at each port on the Neighbor Islands, and most of these were corrupt or incompetent. Before 1882, the entire service employed only one inspector. By 1891, there were a couple dozen, but the personnel records show that of the 79 men employed over the next seven years as customs inspectors, almost one-third were fired for causes such as "stealing," "refusing duty," "insubordination" and "criminal negligence." About half of the 147 men hired as customs guards or night inspectors were fired for "want of confidence," being "asleep-drunk," "drunk and neglecting duty" or merely for being "worthless."

That's what Cleghorn had to work with, and he knew how vulnerable the kingdom was to smugglers. In 1891, with the whole *Halcyon-Claudine* episode still painfully fresh in his mind, he wrote in his annual report that he was "helpless to prevent smuggling" and pleaded for funds. A year later, he sadly chided the legislature that it hadn't given him any more money and the situation hadn't improved.

Cleghorn had inherited the customs job from John M. Kapena, a crony of King Kalākaua, whose personal problems—bankruptcy, the recent death of his wife and a bad case of alcoholism—caused him to neglect the customs service. Kapena had been in charge during the short period in 1887–88 when the monopoly was in force and opium was legal. Cleghorn took over at the tail end of the monopoly period, running the place efficiently, if ineffectively, since then.

Like the United States, Hawaii relied heavily on customs duties and tariffs on exports (mainly sugar) for government revenues, so Cleghorn's job was an important one, and he took it seriously. He knew what needed to be done; he just didn't have the tools to do it. He got a little good news on May 5, when the *Claudine* turned up safe and sound but empty-handed. It hadn't been sunk after all, and those reports of shots fired were exaggerations; unable to find *Halcyon* or anything else interesting, the bored crew had engaged in a little target practice before heading for home. By the time *Claudine* got back to port, there were no further sightings of the dark schooner, so Cleghorn and Wilson sent their rented revenue cutter back into the merchant trade and set the inspectors to searching incoming ships from Asia and the West Coast. One of those inspectors wasn't giving up quite so easily, though.

Billy Sheldon was at it again, moving carefully through the darkness, the crashing of the surf pounding on the beach nearby covering the noise he made as he pushed through the underbrush. The burly customs officer with a grudge against opium peddlers had a lantern but couldn't use it; there were no lights of any kind on this remote stretch of Oahu's Waianae Coast, twenty miles northwest of Honolulu. And Sheldon was trespassing on land leased by the man he was hunting, someone he did not want to alert before he had all of his evidence in hand. That evidence, hundreds of pounds of opium, his informer told him, had been offloaded from *Halcyon* onto a plantation rented by George Lycurgus.

After considerable searching, Sheldon found the spot the informer described, pulling aside the canvas tarpaulin and uncovering the pile of tins beneath. He didn't need the lantern to read the labels or recognize his find—Lai Yuen opium, three hundred tins at least, and maybe a lot more.

Satisfied that the information had checked out, he carefully replaced the canvas, making sure he'd left no sign of his visit. He retreated through the bushes and banana trees toward town, a long ride on horseback and by train ahead of him, but he had a plan; he'd be returning with help to stake out the cache, and when Lycurgus showed up to collect his opium, Sheldon would be waiting.

DEPUTY-SHERIFF SHELDON.

William Sheldon. Nemesis of opium smugglers in Hawaii—and Whaley and George Lycurgus in particular—customs officer and deputy sheriff Sheldon made the largest seizure of *Halcyon*'s opium in early 1891. Pacific Commercial Advertiser.

Before doing anything else, Sheldon had to check in with higher authority and with the police. Customs man Sheldon could seize contraband at the pier or on ships, but he was going to need a sheriff's deputy to assist with arrests or taking opium that had already been landed in Waianae. Here, though, he got his first hint of a problem with his plan. The higher authority he checked in with wasn't nearly as excited as he was about the big opium find. "Don't do anything for a day or two" was a direct order, and while Sheldon fumed and cooled his heels in Honolulu, anything could be happening out in Waianae.

By the time Sheldon got back there with backup two days later, the tins and the tarp were both gone, and all he found was an empty hole. For Sheldon and his stool pigeon, who had both anticipated a big arrest and a sizable reward from the seizure, this was a major disappointment, but it got worse. George Lycurgus, somebody who already walked around Honolulu like he owned the place, came up to Sheldon on the street and taunted him about the missing dope, demanding that Sheldon tell him who had squealed on the stash. Thoroughly convinced that he had been sold out by his own superiors, Sheldon resolved to be more careful in the future. At least he didn't have to wonder how high the corruption went. He'd reported Lycurgus's opium cache to only one person, a friend of William Whaley, Charlie Wilson, the marshal of the kingdom himself.

Aboard *Halcyon*, there was a sense of relief. The opium had all been offloaded on Lanai and at Waianae on Oahu, and the schooner yacht could finally turn toward Victoria after sixteen long and very eventful months. They weren't home free yet. Tommy Evans had told Metcalf and his crew about the reception waiting for them on the Pacific Coast; the San Francisco papers were buzzing about the San Diego crew of the schooner *Fear Naught*, who had put to sea several weeks earlier in hopes of intercepting *Halcyon* as it approached the coast. With twenty heavily armed men aboard, the *Fear Naught*, described in the papers as a "privateer" but legally nothing more than a pirate, had perhaps one chance in ten thousand of encountering *Halcyon*, but after two wrecks, Metcalf was a careful captain and didn't intend to risk even that. He put the schooner on a course that took it due north to catch the favorable winds that would carry it east to Victoria and far out of the reach of *Fear Naught* and any American revenue cutters that might be on the prowl. They were really the ones that had naught to fear. Even if the customs or revenue cutter men caught up with them, *Halcyon* now sailed in ballast. There was no longer any contraband to find.

In Honolulu, Will Whaley and Ewen McLean had loose ends to clean up. Whaley had arrived in town from Yokohama on March 11, well ahead of *Halcyon*, connecting with Lycurgus, who arrived from San Francisco a week later, and Evans, who rented the Waikiki property (now the parking lot for the Honolulu Zoo) for use as a local headquarters for the group. McLean came to help with on March 31, just in time to catch *Halcyon*'s Lanai entrance. He didn't stay long, just a week, lining up the Chinese customers and negotiating the best deals for the three tons of opium about to be dumped into the Honolulu market before returning on April 7 aboard the SS *Australia*.

Whaley was supposed to go with McLean but stayed on, stretching his Hawaii visit on through April and into May. He needed the time to deal with the fallout from Evans's arrest and to make sure that *Halcyon* got cleanly away from the islands. He finally sailed for San Francisco on May 8, aboard the SS *Alameda*, but he wouldn't be gone long. Will Whaley had developed a real fondness for Honolulu. He planned on coming back and staying for a while.

16

A SHOW OF MAINTAINING THE LAW

Back in Honolulu, the newspapers took note of the drop in opium prices, commenting on the sudden popularity of trunks coming from the almost uninhabited island of Lanai and wondering coyly what this mysterious luggage could contain, with broad hints that they knew the answer. The papers also reported on the increasing numbers of arrests, mostly of Chinese men, for possession of opium. Marshal Charles Wilson's police officers were on the job and making life difficult for the small-time opium sellers and users. Meanwhile, those at the top of the traffic (and the newsmen dropped more hints that they knew the identities of these people) were "handled gently." One of Wilson's detractors alleged, "He had pounced upon Chinamen to keep up a show of maintaining the law—some little Chinamen; but the great sinners were let go." This charge would be repeated later, when Charlie Wilson's conduct would be held against the woman he served, the queen of Hawaii, Lili'uokalani.

Those bigger fish at the top of the trade, including the Camarinos brothers operating out of their California Fruit Market on the corner of Alakea and King Streets in downtown Honolulu, began selling the *Halcyon* opium on the wholesale plan. Wilson's police did make a seizure of a couple hundred tins from the Camarinos "ranch" in nearby Kalihi Valley, but as usual, they couldn't tie the opium to anyone, so they didn't prosecute either of the Camarinos boys. Lycurgus's role is less clear. He might have assisted with the offloading and the transportation end of the business, but try as he might, and he tried mightily, Billy Sheldon never caught the Spartan in possession of opium.

Queen's marshal Charles B. Wilson. *Archives of Hawaii.*

Justice came fairly quickly to Thomas Evans. In his May trial in police court, a judge found him guilty of possession of opium and sentenced him to a year at hard labor at Oahu Prison and a $500 fine, which made Billy Sheldon, who'd be getting half of that money, happy. Evans appealed the verdict, saying he wanted a trial by a jury and loudly proclaiming he'd had no idea that the trunks contained opium. The main news from the trial, though, was that Evans was keeping his mouth shut about his friends. At least for the time being, he didn't have anything to say about the rest of the opium ring.

With Hawaii behind *Halcyon* and the green mountains of British Columbia finally in sight ahead, the ship's longest voyage was almost over. On May 23, it arrived at Barclay Sound on Vancouver Island, clearing customs at Victoria on the 25th. Metcalf reported to the customs house that he'd arrived direct from Yokohama with nothing to declare. The inspection verified the claim, and the next day, he filed his papers with the American consul, taking care of the documentation for his American crewmen and himself. Alfred Metcalf's career as *Halcyon*'s captain was over at last, and although it wasn't obvious at the time, this was the moment that the ring began to break. It was also the day that Alfred Metcalf disappeared for four years. He would not come back into view until 1895.

A life in obscurity was not in the cards for Will Whaley, who checked into his old stomping grounds at the Baldwin Hotel and promptly met with interested reporters. He didn't say much. *Halcyon* will be arriving shortly at Victoria, he told them, and it made the cruise to Japan and back in ballast. Apparently, it was all just a sixteen-month pleasure trip. He went north a few days later, giving out more interviews to the British Columbia media, which was even more skeptical about *Halcyon*'s purposeless transpacific wanderings, but Whaley didn't drift off the cover story. "She cleared in ballast and she came back the same way."

"But what about the cargo?" a reporter asked.

"There's nothing to show we ever had a cargo aboard," Whaley told him, which was one of the truest lies he ever spoke.

A crewman also obliged one of the reporters with an interview, saying that they'd "touched sides" with the schooner *Fear Naught*, transferring three hundred "ginger jars" full of opium to the shipload of vigilantes who were supposedly out hunting *Halcyon*. The wag's tall tale, calculated to cause trouble for the *Fear Naught* and its crew, is the only admission from any of *Halcyon*'s crew that there was ever opium on the voyage from Japan.

Nobody, not the reporters, not the customs men in the United States or Canada and not the readers, believed a word of this nonsense, but the effect of this publicity was still significant. The *Halcyon* and the opium ring made for very interesting reading, and it created headlines up and down the coast and clear across the United States as other newspapers eagerly picked up the story. The black schooner and its tall tale were on newspaper pages read by millions, and this is the sort of publicity that criminal organizations generally (and smuggling rings in particular) usually try to avoid.

Will Whaley, with his flamboyant personality and his flair for lighting up a room, knew this but didn't care. He headed south, turning his attention back to Hawaii, where there was opium to sell and money to collect. In July 1891, he boarded the SS *Zealandia* and sailed for Honolulu. He left McLean in Victoria to tidy up after him—no easy job—and McLean, abandoned by his captain, stiffed by his partner and stuck with a boat that was hotter than a Hawaiian volcano, decided to set his sights a little lower, taking *Halcyon* back into the coasting trade and leaving the transoceanic trips behind for a while. The Hong Kong–Honolulu run had, in theory, been fabulously profitable, but until Whaley sold all the dope and collected all the debts, that money remained pie-in-the-sky.

The crew had to be paid, that was the law, and McLean came up with enough money to send cook Constantine Capilos back to San Francisco. It appears he stiffed the others, but mate Jim Harvey said he'd stick with *Halcyon* for another cruise, and his good buddy Bill Johnson stayed too. The Me and Bill partnership would not be broken, even by death, it seemed, something that fate would arrange. Joe Lippett signed off, going back to his wife in Victoria and giving up the sea, becoming a longshoreman. McLean would in time pick up a new captain from the Victoria waterfront, the newsmen watching and reporting every move, but for now, while he waited for Whaley to get the money together, he was lying low. Those good old days, when the gang was all together, the money rolled in and everybody could operate fairly anonymously, were apparently long gone. McLean must have seen that handwriting on the wall. He sailed south for San Francisco, leaving *Halcyon* to swing idly at its mooring by the Point Ellice Bridge in Victoria's harbor, Bill Johnson and his dog aboard, waiting for a call that might never come.

17

A NEAR THING

CLOSE CALL FOR THE OPIUM RING

Whaley blew back into town in July 1891 aboard the SS *Zealandia*, almost instantly "going native" and taking up an island lifestyle that would last him the next fifteen months in Honolulu. His stay started off with an island tradition, the giving of gifts, and Will didn't go for something skimpy like a flower lei. No, his present was an Irish setter puppy, a purebred descendant of a Chicago champion, a $250 pooch that he handed over to a good pal he'd made on his earlier trip to Hawaii. Marshal Charles B. Wilson was overwhelmed; $250 bought a lot of dog in 1891. The marshal reciprocated by giving Whaley a valuable gift in return—a badge and commission in the "marshal's secret police service," something that let the smuggler hang around the police station and purchase a certain amount of immunity. The marshal and Will Whaley became the best of buddies, dining, drinking and playing pool together.

Working with Tommy Evans, who was out on bail pending his appeal, Whaley began collecting some of the opium debts that were due and selling opium. He leased a cottage on Beretania Street, later moving to the place Tommy Evans had been renting in Waikiki, a bungalow called Manuia Lanai, located about a block from the beach near Kapiolani Park. This place already had some history; author Robert Louis Stevenson rented it a year or so before for his visit to the islands.

Whaley adopted a colonial look when it came to dress, favoring white trousers, shirts and coats, with a signature white Panama hat or a pith helmet, everything offset by a colorful silk sash, that flamboyant walrus

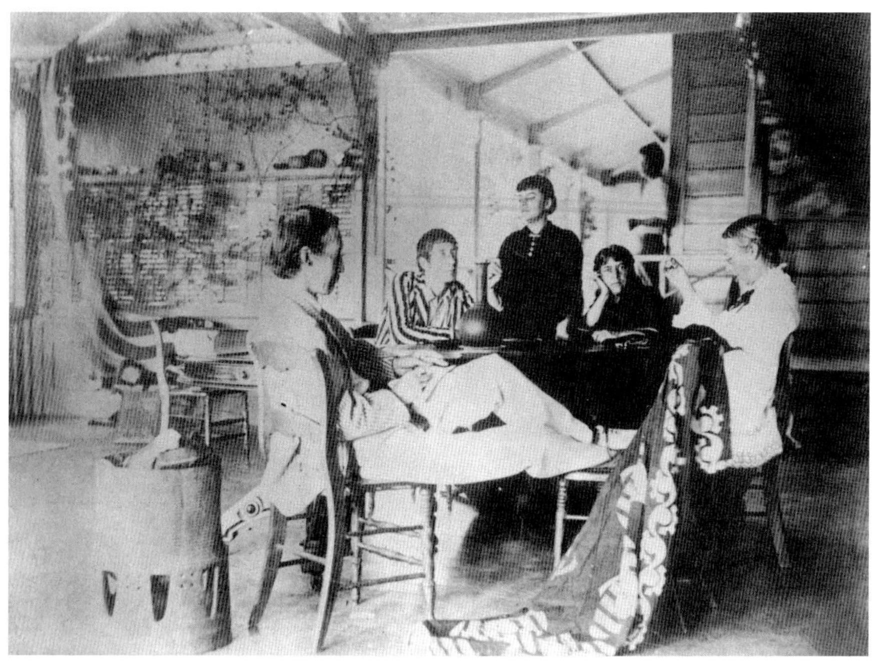

Manuia Lanai. Thomas Evans and William Whaley rented a Waikiki cottage, where William Sheldon seized a trunk full of Halcyon opium. The man seated with his feet up is author Robert Louis Stevenson. *1889, Wikimedia.*

moustache and a big cigar. The life of the party, Whaley hosted a few at his Waikiki place, favoring champagne and buying fresh fruit, meats and vegetables from the Greeks to supply his guests. Honolulu found him to be a great host, and he included Evans, Lycurgus and the Camarinos brothers in the festivities, which also featured fireworks on occasion.

Newspaper reporters, notably Frank L. Hoogs from the *Pacific Commercial Advertiser*, kept an annoyingly close eye on Whaley and reported his activities every chance they got. Like most of his reading public in Honolulu, Hoogs knew Whaley by reputation and knew why he was in town. The only uncertainty, really, was whether Whaley was there to take care of unfinished business from *Halcyon*'s last run or to set things up for the next one. As the weeks passed and 1891 waned, it began to look more and more like he might not be doing much of either, but everyone agreed that he sure could throw a party.

Two blocks away, Thomas Evans got another day in court. Sentenced by a lower court judge to a year at hard labor at Oahu Prison, known in Honolulu as the Reef, Evans had asked for a jury trial, and he got a good

William A. Whaley. An April 1892 photograph of the smuggler during his time in Honolulu. Pacific Commercial Advertiser.

one, persuading twelve of his peers that those trunks from Lanai that arrived at his house were a complete mystery to him. Billy Sheldon's testimony came for naught. Evans won an acquittal, leaving him to brag on the courthouse steps that he'd beaten the rap, strongly implying that he'd been guilty after all. Double jeopardy prevented him from being tried again, much to Sheldon's disgust. This must have come as a big relief to Whaley, as it removed the potential threat that an incarcerated Evans would talk to the government and implicate his partners in the smuggling scheme. Now the only loss was the 280 tins originally seized by Sheldon, so the Evans case represented only a minor hiccup in Whaley's smoothly functioning operation.

Things weren't functioning quite as smoothly as Ewen McLean would have liked, however. Back in San Francisco, the weeks turned into months, and the Hawaii steamers kept pulling into port like clockwork with no sign of Will Whaley or, more importantly, all of the ring's money. The boys were keeping track of Whaley; it wasn't hard, as Hoogs and the other reporters commented frequently on the smuggler's mostly social doings in town, none of which seemed to have anything to do with collecting money and going home to California with it. McLean's investors—Wichman, Greenwald, Thomas, Joslyn and A.J. Smith—frequently reminded him that debts were due and owing.

It had already been more than eighteen months since everybody put up their original shares, and the opium had finally been delivered in April 1891. Almost a full year later, McLean had heard enough whining, and his own patience had run out. In March 1892, the members of the hui met at Greenwald's room on Powell Street in San Francisco. Some tough accusations were thrown around, and McLean didn't like the idea that he'd be held responsible for bringing in the other investors, especially since he was losing money on the deal too. Everybody agreed on one key point: The King of the Opium Ring, Will Whaley, was at the root of all the trouble.

Smith, Greenwald and Wichman headed down to Honolulu with murder on their minds. The gang agreed. If Whaley didn't come up with the money, he was to be "put up," or killed, by the three, who would then work with the other members of the ring, Evans, Lycurgus and the Camarinos brothers, to come up with the money owed them. The three would-be killers boarded the SS *Australia*, arriving in Honolulu on April 19. The murder plot immediately began to fall apart.

One suspects that they might have been angry with Whaley, but none of the three were really murderers at heart. Or maybe they, like so many others before and since, were lulled into mellow complacency by the islands' beauty and tranquility. Or maybe Will Whaley, who sweet-talked the Japanese into giving back his three tons of opium, hadn't lost that golden touch of his and could still talk his way out of a sticky situation. Introducing Wichman, Greenwald and Smith to his good buddy Marshal of the Kingdom Charles Wilson was a not-so-subtle hint that murdering somebody with a direct connection to the chief of police of a foreign country and who held a commission as a special officer might not be such a good plan.

In any event, Whaley showed his three murderers a grand old time in Honolulu, taking them out to fine restaurants; a photographer's studio, where they were all photographed in Chinese costume and wearing leis; and various tourist attractions on the island. At the end of a whirlwind week, Whaley took the three slightly dazed Californians back to the pier and waved aloha as they sailed off into the sunrise aboard the SS *Australia*, not so much as a penny wealthier than when they'd arrived.

A bemused Ewen McLean met them at steamer pier, taking Greenwald home while George Thomas, another investor, did the same for his friend Wichman. Smith went home alone, but they all agreed to meet at Greenwald's apartment the next day. With McLean there, they tried to explain what had happened. McLean heard them out and then told his sheepish henchmen, "You are fine fellows. I sent you to Honolulu to do that fellow up and you did not do it." Although they kept a close watch on each steamer arriving from Honolulu, none of them really expected to see Whaley in California again any time soon, and discussions turned to new smuggling runs, going back to the old tried and true Victoria–San Francisco line. Hawaii, despite all its promise, had been a colossal flop.

18
AND TWO MONARCHS FALL

As the weeks turned into months, Will Whaley partied. The press eagerly reported on his dinner soirees and evening entertainments, speculating that the fireworks displays from Whaley's Waikiki Beach house covered signals to *Halcyon* as it hovered offshore. But anyone who checked could have found the schooner 2,600 miles away at its mooring in Victoria harbor until July 1892. Whaley's nightly excursions to Honolulu's pool halls and night spots also got coverage, especially when he met up with Charlie Wilson for a game of pool or a few drinks. He was still partying and hobnobbing with the elite. In March, he attended a royal ball and met Queen Liliʻuokalani at Iolani Palace.

These were perilous times for the queen, who faced fierce opposition to her favored legislation in what became the longest legislature in Hawaiian history. Two of the more contentious bills were efforts by the queen to raise money independent of the businessmen, factors and bankers who controlled the kingdom's finances. One measure would have licensed a lottery using Hawaii's postal system to sell tickets in the United States. The second would have created a monopoly for the sale of opium. Whaley had his hands on both. He and Evans were closely associated with two of the lottery promoters, John Phillips and Dr. Gilbert Foote, a California physician. Whaley and the Greeks and Tommy Evans parceled their opium out and kept the money rolling in as the weeks turned into months and the longest legislative session in Hawaiian history drew to its bitter conclusion.

Iolani Palace—home in 1892 of Queen Lili'uokalani, destined to be Hawaii's last monarch. *Bancroft Library, University of California, Berkeley.*

The hidden hand behind these machinations was no longer around to see it, however. By October 1892, Will Whaley had finally collected enough money from the sale of the *Halcyon* opium—probably between $75,000 and $150,000 ($2.1 to $4.25 million in 2020 dollars)—that he felt comfortable taking the next big step. On October 4, he boarded a departing ship, the SS *China,* and sailed away from Hawaii forever. But he wasn't headed for San Francisco and a reckoning with the other members of his opium ring. The *China* was bound for Yokohama, Japan. Needless to say, he took all the money with him.

He took a friend, too, Dr. Gilbert Foote of the lottery scheme, and Whaley never looked back. Three months later, in January 1893, White businessmen, lawyers and planters, with the (at least) tacit support of sailors and marines from the USS *Boston,* overthrew Queen Lili'uokalani and proclaimed a provisional government in Hawaii, pending annexation of the islands by the United States.

Whaley's co-conspirator A.J. Smith, writing later, said that George Lycurgus had supported the lottery with bribe money and the queen had promised him a high position in government, even the marshal's job itself. That claim is doubtful, but Whaley and the Greeks might have seen legal

Queen Lili'uokalani. *Library of Congress.*

opium in Hawaii as a golden opportunity. Never mind the domestic market, the local Chinese, like Chun Afong, could keep that. The islands could be the hub that served San Francisco, Portland, Seattle, Panama and Tahiti. From a legal perch in the mid-Pacific, the King of the Opium Ring could leave Victoria and its factories, 2,400 miles farther from Hong Kong, in the dust. It was a compelling picture but only ever a pipe dream, after all.

What's odd is that neither Whaley and his opium dream nor Foote and his lottery scheme stayed to find out how their fantasies ended, leaving three months before the bills were even voted on. Whaley took the money and ran. Foote, who was along for the ride, sickened in Japan, returned to Honolulu, got worse, went home to California and died there in 1894. The new government quickly repealed both the opium and lottery bills and never issued an opium license. The Louisiana State Lottery Company turned south to Honduras, buying its franchise there, but it was forced underground after 1893 in the United States and gradually went bust.

19

THE KING IS DEAD

LONG LIVE THE KING

The year 1891 cracked the opium ring. Metcalf set sail for ports unknown, saying goodbye to his ship for good. The year 1892 saw Whaley abscond with all of the money from the Hawaii run—two full years' worth of planning, work and $100,000 in investor profits gone with him and two widows to Japan. *Halcyon* was as hot as an opium lamp, making headlines even without leaving its berth in Victoria. Ewen McLean was no quitter, though; all those smokers in San Francisco needed their opium, and the Chinese merchants paying for the show needed the money the addicts were willing to pay. By the time Will Whaley sailed away on the SS *China*, McLean had made new plans and taken steps to carry them out.

The new king started fresh, though he still had Me and Bill—mate Jim Harvey and seaman Bill Johnson. Sailors were a dime a dozen in Victoria; eager men lined up for a chance to crew on the opium runner, but McLean was picky, going with known quantities as a reflection of his conservatism. He needed a captain and finally found one, Charles Johnson, a Victoria man, and Johnson had no trouble filling out the crew. Meanwhile, McLean was finding that being king came with some problems.

His biggest problem was that *Halcyon* was famous—not just in Victoria and Honolulu and San Francisco but also all over the United States. People with newspapers in Kansas and Maine and Arizona were reading stories about the schooner and its opium cargo and wondering where it would turn up next. Newspaper reporters gathered around *Halcyon* at the pier, asking when it would be leaving and how much opium it'd have aboard. Then they wrote the noncommittal answers in the next edition of the paper. Spies and snitches and stool pigeons watched *Halcyon* and the crew's every move. It couldn't change berths in the harbor without twenty people reporting it to the American and Hawaiian consulates in Victoria. McLean knew that if *Halcyon* was going to complete any more successful runs, he'd have to make some changes.

He started with a familiar misdirection, making a public announcement that he'd put the schooner up for sale, claiming he'd been forced to do so to pay twenty-nine months in back wages for his crew. This didn't fool anybody, but he went ahead with the plan, which was to leave port empty and collect the opium and a large group of Chinese immigrants somewhere in Barclay Sound. *Halcyon*'s new master filed the appropriate papers with Canadian customs, declaring it was clearing in ballast, and at the end of July 1892, it slipped out of port.

The first part of the plan went well, as *Halcyon* picked up two and a half tons of opium and nineteen Chinese immigrants before heading out into the Pacific. That was really the only thing the ship had going for it; no one besides McLean and the crew knew its destination. Customs in San Francisco was on the lookout and sent men out to other California ports, but they didn't have anybody at Monterey Bay, which is where the schooner appeared out of the darkness.

Everything went well at first, with the opium safely landed and most of the Chinese but then they lost the boat in the surf and a man drowned. Monterey police caught some of the aliens, and the next day, a train flattened another Chinese man as he tried to retrieve his trunk from the railroad tracks. When police opened the dead man's trunk, they found it full of opium tins.

By the time the customs men arrived, *Halcyon* had gone again, its boat left behind, but this last run hadn't panned out, with most of the Chinese caught. Worse, news of the commotion in Monterey got back to Victoria, upsetting the customs authorities there. They intercepted *Halcyon* when it crossed back into Canadian waters, searching it, finding nothing but hauling it to Victoria. After some consideration, they slapped the ship with an $800 fine for failing to follow clearing papers. It was a technical violation, but it sent as clear a message as possible that the Canadian government had had about as much of *Halcyon* as it was going to take. McLean got the hint. He announced that he'd put the schooner up for sale, and this time it was true.

He got a buyer quickly enough, the E.B. Marvin Company of Victoria, which hauled the ship out, putting it high and dry on the marine railway and tending to the bottom, which had started growing bumper crops of weed and barnacles, and began getting it ready for a new trade. It would be called *Vera* now, and it'd be a sealer. The most notorious opium smuggler of the age was no more. Marvin had paid $5,200 for *Halcyon*, almost exactly what Whaley and Mclean paid Grant and Morrow in 1887.

Over the next twenty years, *Vera* made a name for itself in the sealing business, and it made it in much the same way it had in the opium trade—on pure speed. It didn't take long for the new captain to establish his ship as the fastest schooner in the Victoria sealing fleet, and that's how things stayed for *Vera*'s whole career. It proved its title more than once in the annual race to the sealing grounds off Japan, though none of the other captains would bet against it. In March 1895, two veteran sealers, the *Agnes Macdonald* and the *E.B. Marvin*, fair flyers themselves, made a $250 wager between them on which would be the first to reach Japan from Victoria, racing across the North Pacific. The *Marvin* drove so hard that it lost its topmast in the press to make port first. It won the race and the $250, but it turned out to be a rather hollow victory. *Vera*, which had left Victoria a *full week after* the other two sealers, arrived at Yokohama three days *before* either boat, writing a new chapter in the *Halcyon* legend.

But having sold *Halcyon* at the end of 1892, McLean needed a new ship and a captain, too. He started by gathering the investors together. They'd all

Schooner *Halcyon* in its later career as *Vera*, moored in Victoria Harbor. *Archives of British Columbia.*

been burned by Will Whaley and now they needed to make some successful runs to get that money back. The easiest way to score was the one tried and true over the past six years—Victoria to San Francisco. They all met at Louis Greenwald's place and divided up the responsibilities for the operation. McLean would be in charge of getting the opium together in Victoria, and they planned to add some income by running some Chinese along with the dope. A.J. Smith's job was to find the ship and put together a crew. He knew the waterfront, so he was the logical choice. The boat didn't have to be as big or as fast as *Halcyon*, but everyone agreed that after Whaley and *Halcyon*, it would be nice if they could keep the new ship's role a secret for a change.

Greenwald would be arranging for the landing of the opium, while George Thomas and George Wichman were brought in as investors, providing money for half of the cargo. McLean arranged through his Chinatown contacts to get the rest on credit from the Victoria opium merchants. The plot took some time to coalesce, but in late Spring, Greenwald found Smith and told him that they were "ready for business." This was Smith's cue to start the hunt for the right ship. He found one in exactly the same place that Whaley and McLean had found *Halcyon*, at the Pacific Yacht Club in Sausalito.

In June 1893, Smith purchased the yacht *Emerald*, a smaller boat than Harry Tevis's schooner at only twenty-one tons, but one familiar on the bay and the Sacramento River. Smith paid $1,225 from Orin Henderson of Stockton, California. With the boat in hand, Smith contracted with *Halcyon*'s builder, William Stone, to make some improvements and ready the little ship for some ocean cruises. In early July, *Emerald* went onto the ways at Stone's shipyard for repairs, and when it was relaunched, Smith purchased provisions for the ship while McLean arranged to buy the opium in Victoria.

Smith also went looking for a crew. He found a captain, John Lockhart, and hired him, but everybody soon agreed that Lockhart wasn't going to work out, as he claimed to be able to foretell storms from conversations with spirits and to hear these spirits aboard *Emerald.* This disconcerted the crew, two men called Gus and Charley who considered him a "hoodoo captain" and forcefully expressed their reluctance to sail under Lockhart's command.

Smith decided to dump the psychic commander and the mutinous sailors and would eventually pick up two more crewmen. Now, he needed a captain again and went looking on the San Francisco waterfront, where he knew master mariners in search of ships could be found. Of course, Smith needed a captain who was also willing to join a smuggling conspiracy, but he was

The opium ring's second ship, also a former yacht, was the speedy little *Emerald*. *Bancroft Library, University of California, Berkeley.*

pretty sure he could find one of those on the Embarcadero, too. Surprisingly, the man he signed up wasn't fresh off some voyage from Sydney or Liverpool but operating a butcher shop in Oakland.

The new master of *Emerald* was a short, portly, silent German who went by the name of Jack Voss. A hard drinker and a mean drunk, John Claus Voss was also one hell of a seaman and exactly the man you wanted in command of a small boat with a valuable cargo on the North Pacific Ocean. Voss had no obvious moral scruples, no objection to smuggling opium (or cold-blooded murder) and, as the ring would discover to its regret, a light-fingered approach toward other people's hard-earned smuggling profits.

Jack Voss had been at sea since he was a teenager, and he worked his way up, finally earning his master's license at age forty, sailing out of the Port of San Francisco. He was taciturn to the point of speechlessness, and it was almost impossible to have a decent conversation with Voss when he was sober. After a few drinks, though, he loosened up and became very jolly and entertaining company. After a few more, the other side of Jack Voss appeared, and people who knew him tended to leave that one alone and at as safe a distance as possible.

With Voss and his new crewmen, mate Charles Mensing and seaman Henry Miller, who would also serve as cook, *Emerald* made a trial trip on July 10, taking McLean, Wichman, Greenwald and Greenwald's girlfriend along for a little shakedown cruise. Voss needed to make some last-minute arrangements; he'd gotten into a little scrape with another vessel, a minor collision that broke *Emerald*'s gaff, but with that repaired and with everything else finally to his satisfaction, *Emerald* set sail for British Columbia on July 14. While the ship was gone, Smith met with McLean, who said there

John Claus Voss. *Emerald*'s captain for its two Victoria–San Francisco smuggling runs. The Venturesome Voyages of Captain Voss.

would be no problem getting the opium and passengers ashore, as he had bribed two customs inspectors. Greenwald was arranging for two boats to land the cargo.

With those arrangements set, McLean took a steamer north for Victoria to see to the opium. He had some help from another old *Halcyon* hand, C.S. Joslyn, who was still living part time in Victoria. Joslyn purchased a half-ton of opium from one of the dozen suppliers in downtown Victoria. Wary of those Canadian customs officers who had given *Halcyon* such a hard time on its last run, McLean and Joslyn decided to avoid the port of Victoria and its custom house altogether, contracting with a vessel to take the opium and eight Chinese to Barclay Sound on the west side of Vancouver Island. There, they could meet up with *Emerald* away from government agents and all those waterfront stool pigeons.

Voss, an efficient captain, made the rendezvous exactly on time and in precisely the right place. In fact, he was early and annoyed when McLean failed to show as promised. Miller described the rendezvous in some detail, saying said Voss groused, "It's a hell of a man who can't keep an appointment," and told Miller to watch for a red light that would signal the meeting.

Miller didn't see anything until they had shifted anchorage and moved up the sound, where they met a large steamer, or at least one larger than *Emerald*. McLean came aboard and transferred thirteen cases marked "Pratt's Astral Oil" and five Chinese. Voss told Miller that "this is our cargo" as the steamer towed them "a little way" and then cut them loose, McLean going back aboard the other ship but not before Voss gave everybody a glimpse of the darker side of his personality. He didn't intend on going to an American prison for this crime, or a Canadian one, either. *Emerald* was no *Halcyon*, able to outrun any pursuers. Captain Voss made it clear to McLean and the others that if challenged, he intended to jettison the cargo, getting rid of any evidence of smuggling before the customs men could seize it.

That meant the opium, but it also included the Chinese immigrants, who were all getting tied up and thrown into the drink with the dope. Since

Voss had no apparent sense of humor and clearly wasn't kidding around, the principals accepted the terms and the possible loss of their cargo and investment. Nobody suggested to the potentially doomed immigrants that they might want to wait for another ship, and Voss set sail, turning *Emerald* south and staying just outside the three-mile limit as he coasted along past Washington and Oregon.

The weather wasn't bad, a bit rugged, but they made their way in fairly good time to the rendezvous point. *Emerald* might not have had *Halcyon*'s speed, but it did have an advantage that the larger, faster ship did not. The little yawl had a centerboard, a flat, heavy metal keel that could be lowered or raised. This allowed *Emerald* to go into much shallower waters, opening up many more possibilities for Voss and his crew. He could take his ship right inshore or up into bays or rivers. Or close inshore at Duxbury Reef, a fairly dangerous point between Drake's Bay and the Golden Gate. McLean, who had taken the steamer south, was waiting with a fishing boat, Greenwald and an offload crew when Voss anchored at about 3:00 p.m. on August 7.

The opium and Chinese went aboard the fishing boat, which sailed off toward San Francisco. McLean stayed aboard *Emerald*, which sailed the next day into San Francisco and tied up near Mission Flats. Smith, who was living in his sister's apartment, which had a view of the bay, saw *Emerald* return on August 8. He went to Wichman's candy store on Market Street, where he met Voss.

The captain said they'd had a rough trip but transferred the one thousand pounds of opium and eight Chinese. (The number disagrees with Miller, who said there were only five.) The next day, Wichman confirmed that everything had been successfully brought to San Francisco.

The smugglers divided up the proceeds, $2,130, although Smith said that he suspected Voss had already helped himself to a cut. Miller, who claimed he hadn't been told until he got to Canada that he was going on a smuggling trip, got $60 for his part, but he was game for another run. The ring planned for it, but *Emerald* needed some work; it had developed a leak and required other repairs. Back onto William Stone's ways she went, A.J. Smith making those arrangements as Miller slept aboard at Hunter's Point.

The second voyage took place in September. *Emerald* went north with the same crew, this time heading a little deeper into Canadian waters. Once again, Voss told Miller to watch for a red light, and this time McLean appeared in a Chinese junk, bringing fifteen "cases" and some sacks with loose tins of opium, as well as thirteen Chinese passengers. *Emerald* was going to be very crowded on this trip south, and Voss wasn't happy about it.

He got unhappier when mate Charles Mensing told Voss to "go to hell, I'm not going down with a lot of Chinese" and jumped ship to McLean's junk. This left *Emerald* dangerously shorthanded, but Voss wasn't giving up.

This was because he had a plan that would put him in a very good mood. He'd learned a lot from all that griping about Will Whaley and his treachery. The most important lesson was that when somebody stole your smuggling profits, there wasn't anything legal you could do about it—no calling the cops or getting a lawyer and going to court. You had to either take your lumps or dish them out. And the second-most important lesson was that this bunch—McLean, Greenwald, Thomas, Wichman and Smith—took their lumps. The opium business was about to have its second big betrayal.

20

THE *EMERALD* RING

Voss and Miller had a rough trip going south, finally making it to the shelter of Point Reyes and Drake's Bay, but they'd lost their small boat and had to deal with sickness among the Chinese passengers. Voss anchored and went looking for their contact, thinking maybe Mensing would be there, giving it one last chance. Mensing was nowhere to be seen, and neither was McLean or anyone else from the ring, so Voss told Miller they were going right into the bay. He meant San Francisco Bay.

On October 1, *Emerald* pulled into its home waters, gliding up to the W.I. Stone boatyard at Hunter's Point. Voss called for a boat, and Stone sent one off as Voss took one of the sacks, telling Miller to keep the Chinese out of sight in the cabin while he went ashore. When Voss returned in another boat that night, he took all of the opium and told Miller to land all of the Chinese. Miller did so and then helped them get aboard trolley cars and took them to Chinatown, watching them scatter in the darkness, their long voyage to the Gold Mountains finally complete. Miller returned to the shipyard, joining Voss in the boat with the opium. Voss said he had a friend in Martinez, who could help dispose of the opium and offered Miller $150 for his help. The two hijackers set off up the bay, abandoning *Emerald*, which Treasury agents found tied up at a pier at Hunter's Point in January 1894.

Their destination was a decrepit bark, the *Southern Chief*, captained by a friend of Voss, August W. Svenson. When Voss pulled alongside, he called for Svenson and said, "I have got some opium and there is some money in it for you." A.W. Svenson didn't hesitate for a minute to join the

Emerald abandoned at Hunter's Point. San Francisco Chronicle.

drug trade. "All right, I'm your man," he replied. All of the opium, 1,300 pounds of it, went aboard the *Southern Chief*, and they stored it below decks. Voss assured Svenson and his nervous wife that they could blame Miller if any of it was discovered and left the cook/seaman/patsy aboard the ship to guard the stash.

When Voss returned a couple days later, he brought an accomplice, the long-absent deserter Charles Mensing, and the two of them and Svenson boxed the opium in crates and barrels marked "Crockery," moving it ashore and disappearing. Miller, broke and owed $75 by the ring, tried to get the money and finally got a few dollars from Mensing, leaving the *Southern Chief* for the city. In San Francisco, he ran into a very upset Ewen McLean and

C.S. Joslyn. They wanted to know where Voss and their opium were and offered Miller $3,000 if he would put them in touch with their former captain. Miller said he didn't know where Voss was and asked for the $75 that he was owed. McLean told him it wasn't his responsibility, something Miller would remember when it came time to choose sides at trial.

While Miller fretted and McLean stewed, Jack Voss was proving to be a much better sea captain than he was a dope dealer. He loaded up a trunk full of opium and took the Southern Pacific train clear to Denver, Colorado, hoping to unload the stolen goods a long way from San Francisco. He didn't have much luck and brought the trunk, still full or almost, all the way back to Sacramento, where he met up with Svenson. Still trying to move the load outside Frisco's Chinatown, they drew the attention of Sacramento's Internal Revenue officer, Horace Byington, whose men seized the trunk and arrested the two sea captains for possession of 179 tins of untaxed opium. The government initially set bail at $3,000, which neither man had a hope of making as the Treasury agents went after the rest of the dope. They had help now, as an informer came to the Appraiser's Building and gave up the entire scheme. Having an insider provide all the details—or at least as many as he knew—gave the special agents a big advantage in putting their case together, and by January, they had most of the picture.

What they didn't have was Jack Voss and August W. Svenson. Shortly after arresting the men, the government moved the case down to San Francisco, and the United States commissioner reduced the bail to $500. Voss and Svenson didn't have that kind of money, either, but they did still have the bulk of 1,300 pounds of opium that the feds hadn't found. Voss cut a deal with McLean to give back the opium in exchange for cash. With bail posted, Voss and Svenson promptly fled California for Victoria as the U.S. attorney prepared an indictment that named the two absent captains, as well as Ewen McLean, C.S. Joslyn, George Wichman, George Thomas, Louis Greenwald, Charles Mensing and Frederick Miller.

The United States marshal went out to round up the gang in January 1894. On January 11, the marshal himself went to McLean's house at 2206 Divisadero Street and had to fight his way past the McLeans' servant girl, who was determined to not let him in. He prevailed but did not find his target, who had fled with Joslyn for British Columbia. The deputies had better luck with the others, bagging everyone else named in the indictment, and this time the commissioner set bail at an amount the men couldn't make. Since the federal government had no prisons in the area, the prisoners went to various state facilities. Miller went to the Alameda

San Francisco photographer and *Halcyon* investor, George N. Thomas also helped finance *Emerald*'s runs. *California State Library.*

County Jail in Oakland. Wichman, Thomas and Greenwald went to the county lockup in San Francisco and then to the state prison at San Quentin. Trial was set for May—a long four months behind those walls for a candy seller and two clerks.

The *Emerald* ring had been a total disaster. McLean told Smith that Joslyn lost $6,000 he'd put into the deal and said Wichman and Thomas had both lost out. Greenwald hadn't lost money, but he certainly wasn't enjoying his new accommodations at San Quentin. Up in Victoria, the indictment barred Voss and Svenson from reentering the United States, something that severely limited their sea captain options. Voss bought a hotel. All of the opium was gone, either stolen or seized by the government, McLean said. It's hard to see how the situation could get any worse. And then it did.

A.J. Smith felt himself used in all of this. He'd now been burned—badly—twice in a row through his association with McLean, Thomas, Wichman and Greenwald. Never mind that he'd been the one who found Voss and brought him into the operation, Smith was convinced that the others had managed to get their investments back, leaving him holding the bag. He also wondered why Ewen McLean was so friendly with the captain who'd ripped him off that he'd floated the thief's bail. Smith carried a particular grudge for George N. Thomas, blaming him for most of his misfortune in both opium rings. Now, A.J. Smith wanted as much revenge as he could get, and he knew exactly where to go to get it. He walked over to the office of Treasury special agent Legare Phenix at the United States Appraiser's Building in San Francisco and started spilling his guts. Since Smith knew all about William Whaley and the *Halcyon* conspiracy, as well as the more recent *Emerald* fiasco, the Treasury men were quite interested in what their new friend had to say.

21

SHATTERED *EMERALD*

They say that hell hath no fury like a woman scorned, but when it came to fury, hell and scorned women had plenty of competition from Albion J. Smith. After getting ripped off by Will Whaley, Smith stuck it out with McLean through *Halcyon*'s last run and then through *Emerald*'s trials. He wanted to get his money back and get ahead, if possible, but somewhere along the line, he gave up that goal and settled on a new one. Now, A.J. Smith just wanted to get even.

When 1894 began, Smith had given the whole *Emerald* story—or as much of it as he knew—to the Treasury agents. He claimed he knew little or nothing about the second load, that he'd been kept in the dark about that one and that was one of the reasons he was so annoyed with the other members of the ring. But he knew a lot. The agents put it together with the Sacramento seizure, along with odds and ends they picked up from people eager to collect any rewards that might be on offer. By January, the grand jury had seen enough and handed down an indictment.

Bringing charges was the easy part for the prosecutor on the case. Samuel Knight III, thirty-one, was a native Californian and a rising star in the state bar. Knight's first problem was that some key defendants—Voss, Svenson, Joslyn and McLean—were still out of reach up in Victoria. Also, unless things changed, Knight's key witness at trial would be A.J. Smith, someone who brought a boatload of baggage with him to the witness stand. Going over the evidence, Knight decided he needed more. He had two investigators assigned to the matter. Special Agent Legare Phenix, forty-four and an attorney, had been a Treasury agent since 1885, appointed in South Carolina but transferred to Sacramento, where he was working Chinese Red Eagle certificate fraud when the *Emerald* matter came up. Phenix was sharp, methodical and a good interviewer and had no problem leaning hard on people he thought could help advance his case.

The second investigator was pushing the matter even before Smith started talking. Peter S. Chappelle, only twenty, a private detective who also held a commission as a deputy U.S. marshal, got onto the ring early, tipped by an informer about *Halcyon* men now sailing another ship. He shadowed members of the ring around town and observed McLean and Greenwald together as they put the conspiracy in motion. He also saw the ringleaders meeting with customs officials Robert Pattison and Charles A. Noyes. This was highly suspicious, especially in light of McLean's boast that he'd bribed two customs men, and the government would later indict Pattison, who had been under investigation before. When the *Emerald* charges came down in January, it was Chappelle who went out to arrest Wichman, Thomas and Greenwald. Now, he and Phenix were looking for other witnesses who could help Knight with the trial.

A shortage of witnesses wasn't Knight's main problem. He already had about fifty. Sailors from the *Southern Chief* could testify about strange men with boxes coming aboard. Orrin Henderson would testify that he sold *Emerald* to A.J. Smith, and William I. Stone would swear that he fixed it up and made it ready for sea. The Internal Revenue officers from Sacramento would tell the jurors about how they'd seized Voss's trunk and the 179 tins of opium and what Voss and Svenson had to say for themselves after their arrests. Knight even had someone to testify about the Canadian source of the opium. All of that was fine, and it would take about a week of the jury's time, but Knight wondered if he had enough to prove knowledge and a conspiracy beyond a reasonable doubt. Like every good prosecutor, he wanted a lead pipe cinch, which meant he needed more.

To get more, he needed to approach the people under indictment and locked up or the ones under indictment and fugitives. Knight was open to both options, and with the trial set for May 1894, he had some time. In March, he dispatched Special Agent Phenix to Victoria to do some negotiating with Voss, Svenson and McLean. The government never publicized what kind of deal it offered, but whatever it was, it wasn't enough. Phenix said both Voss and McLean were interested and talkative but refused to return to the United States without solid assurances of absolute immunity. Sensibly, the assistant U.S. attorney didn't think giving the ringleaders a free pass was a particularly good deal for the United States of America, and he wired Phenix to come back to San Francisco alone.

That left the people in jail or on bail. As it gets closer to trial time, doubts always begin to creep into defendants' minds. Is it better to take your chances with a jury or cut a deal with the government? In 1894, the prosecutors offered extremely good bargains in exchange for testimony. In the Red Eagle case, Champagne Billy Boyd walked away with a free pass. And not only had he been a key player, but he had also fled the jurisdiction before coming back to take the deal. Knight and the government had at least one of these sweet offers for lower-ranking men of the *Emerald* ring, and although mate Charles Mensing was adamant about going all the way to a jury verdict, others were undoubtedly weighing their options as March and April passed.

Knight developed a trial strategy he hoped would make up for the lack of insider information. It relied on the aura and reputation of another opium smuggler who wouldn't be in attendance that month. Since just about everybody in San Francisco had heard about Whaley and the *Halcyon*, the government's lawyers thought they could pile a little guilt by association on at least three of the men who would be sitting at the defense table.

Greenwald, Wichman and Thomas had been up to their necks in the *Halcyon* ring, and Smith certainly knew all about that one. And as May got closer, A.J. Smith, with revenge on his mind, was just aching to testify.

Also aching was former *Emerald* seaman and cook Frederick Miller. He didn't like it in the Alameda County Jail, where his mother and sister visited him and he couldn't get anything to drink. He had a lot of free time in his cell to think about things, and the more he thought about them, the more it seemed that he'd gotten a bad deal in this scheme. Jack Voss, who'd asked him into the operation, was living free in Canada. Ewen McLean, who wouldn't even pay him the $75 they owed him for crewing his last trip, likewise. Furthermore, all of his co-defendants had managed to post their bails, which had been set at $5,000 each—astronomical for the time—leaving just Miller locked up to await trial. The lowliest man on the entire *Emerald* totem pole, he'd gotten less money out of more work than anybody else in the whole scheme. He complained about this to his mother and a friend. His friend talked to the Treasury men and relayed Miller's story. He also told them that Miller had a serious drinking problem, a weakness that Legare Phenix thought might be worked to the government's advantage.

As the date for picking a jury drew near, the two sides sparred with each other, mostly huffing and puffing, neither as confident about their cases as they pretended in public. Rumors that Voss was coming back and giving up the whole scheme floated about and rattled the defense cages. It certainly wasn't beyond the realm of possibility. Anybody who knew Jack Voss knew he wouldn't hesitate ten seconds before stabbing someone in the back if he thought there was something in it for him. But the defense attorneys weren't too worried. By the time they were through with him on cross examination, the jurors would know the real Jack Voss, and the lawyers were betting they wouldn't like him, either.

Federal district judge William Morrow scheduled trial to begin on May 8, 1894, but it was postponed for a day as the government moved to increase everyone's bail to $10,000 ($300,000 in 2021 dollars) and announced a major surprise. The defendants had more reasons to run today, Knight told the court. Last Friday, he and Phenix had interviewed Frederick Miller, who had finally come around. Miller made a complete statement, a full confession, giving up the whole scheme. The other defendants looked shocked and upset at the news, which was about to get worse.

Judge Morrow had some experience with these kinds of cases. He'd been a special agent with the Treasury Department himself, working "confidential assignments" in California for four years. He'd also been an attorney in

Emerald ring defendants in court. A courtroom sketch artist for the *San Francisco Call* drew the four men on trial in the *Emerald* conspiracy. San Francisco Call.

private practice and an assistant United States attorney who handled opium cases in which the defendants skipped bail and disappeared, so he understood how the world worked. He granted the motion to double the bail. Nobody could raise the extra cash, and everybody went back into custody. Round one went to the prosecution.

On May 9, the attorneys spent all day picking a jury. They went through thirty potential jurors before settling on the twelve they wanted. With the day gone, Judge Morrow set opening statements for 11:00 a.m. on May 10, giving Phenix and Knight another evening to prepare their newest witness for his ordeal on the stand. That Thursday morning saw a packed courtroom for San Francisco's trial of the year, if not the decade, and Assistant U.S. Attorney Knight began his opening statement not with the *Emerald*'s story but with Will Whaley's.

More accurately, he began with the failed effort by McLean, Greenwald, Wichman and Smith to get Whaley to pay the money owed them for *Halcyon*'s ill-fated Hawaii run. He explained how the loss of everyone's *Halcyon* investment led to the decision to try another run or two with another ship, how McLean "favored San Francisco as the Chinese at Honolulu could not be trusted." Knight described McLean as the leader and outlined how the *Emerald* was purchased and made two trips in June and September 1893. Knight explained all of this, the government would prove, and that the four men sitting at the defense table conspired to make it happen beyond a reasonable doubt.

Then, and not a minute too soon to suit the revenge minded A.J. Smith, it was the former conspirator's turn to explain just how badly he'd been "done up" by McLean, Greenwald, Thomas and Wichman. Lead-off witness Smith got right down to work. He began saying he'd first met Greenwald at D.G. Camarinos's fruit store in March 1892. In about April of that year, he, Wichman and Greenwald sailed to Honolulu on the SS *Australia* and met with Whaley, returning a week later on the same ship. Frustrated in their efforts to recover their investment from Whaley, they "changed the current of the conversation and they talked of running opium into this port." The suggestion was made by McLean, who favored San Francisco.

Smith continued:

> *It was about this time that I decided that they had done me up for $2,500 on a previous transaction. It was to get back this money that we went to Honolulu. I was determined to get even. In the new scheme McLean was to go to Victoria and arrange for securing the opium and Chinese.*

> *Thomas and Wichman were to furnish the money and Greenwald was to see to landing the contraband Chinese and opium here. Some Chinese merchants in Chinatown were to arrange for McLean getting credit among their countrymen at Victoria. We figured that we could get $85 apiece for bringing the Chinamen down. Thomas, Wichman and others who advanced the money were to receive 40 percent of the profits.*

Smith told how he'd found *Emerald* and a captain, John Lockhart, the oddball psychic. The yacht cost $1,225, $750 in cash and a note for the balance. Smith got $600 from McLean and $150 from Wichman, becoming a boat owner. They made some sea trials that uncovered some problems, fired the captain and crew and hired Voss away from his butcher's shop in Oakland, getting the whole show ready to go by mid-July. Smith claimed that his intention all along was to bring *Emerald* back down from Victoria with its load of opium and aliens, at which time he would turn the whole thing over to the authorities.

That was a good story and very convenient at this point, but when *Emerald* disappeared beyond the Golden Gate, Smith effectively lost control of it. He'd only find out *Emerald* returned when someone told him or if he happened to see it come into port. He did see the ship come into the bay, on August 8, watching the little yawl pass within fifty yards of Meiggs Wharf. He went to see Wichman to find out what was up and discovered Voss already at the candy shop. The captain said they'd had a rough trip but landed one thousand pounds of opium and thirteen Chinese. The next day, Smith met again with Wichman, who said everything had gone well with the opium and aliens landed successfully.

Shown a photo of Voss, Smith identified it. He said he didn't have any other contact with the smugglers until October, when he went looking for them and found McLean, who said *Emerald* was overdue and might be lost on another run. At the end of October, McLean told him that Voss had "run away with the stuff" and had been caught at Sacramento with a man named Svenson. McLean said he'd helped bail the two out, putting down another $700. Thoroughly disgusted with the whole lot of them, he said, Smith headed down to the Appraiser's Building and sought out Special Agent Phenix. With this, Sam Knight was finished.

Prosecutor Knight now produced a series of boring but necessary witnesses who would bolster Smith's testimony, people who could corroborate the signing of the bill of sale for the yacht, tradesmen who supplied *Emerald* with water and other supplies and Orrin S. Henderson of Stockton, who confirmed that he'd sold *Emerald* to Smith. The defense mostly let these witnesses come and go without comment. None of them could put opium in their clients' hands or prove a conspiracy existed. Most of them had never even seen their clients, so they were best quickly forgotten.

Friday morning saw another packed courtroom, everyone anticipating fireworks as one co-conspirator turned on the others. Prosecutor Knight put the moment off, however, leading with a few more of those witnesses who corroborated Smith's story or would be backing up Miller when he took the stand. Before that, however, spectators witnessed what must be one of the oddest scenes ever to take place in a federal courthouse. Modern Americans will scarcely believe it actually happened, as the United States government's official opium smoker took the stand and smoked up some opium right there in front of the whole assemblage.

Mun Jin Moy brought his gear with him, a bamboo opium pipe, a lamp and the tools necessary to heat the opium in the lamp's flame. Reporters commented on how well-worn the pipe appeared, having "turned from a light yellow to a rich mahogany hue." Mun obviously had plenty of practice and definitely qualified as an expert witness. The government selected 6 five-tael tins from the 179 seized from Voss by Internal Revenue at Sacramento, and Moy prepared pills from these tins and "cooked his dope over the little spirit lamp, and then, placing it on the bowl of the pipe, sucked away with apparently great enjoyment as his little eyes blinked and glistened through the wreaths of smoke."

The government's official opium smoker. Expert witness Mun Jin Moy tests the government's opium in the *Emerald* conspiracy trial. San Francisco Chronicle, *May 12, 1894.*

Mun considered carefully. "Him velly good," he said and ruled that the opium had come from Victoria, being a higher quality than that from Panama. This demonstration took place in open court but without the jury present. Mun would testify to his official conclusion on the prosecution's last day, in what passes for 1894's version of a CSI laboratory report. Having been paid by the federal government to get high on the taxpayer dime, not to mention the government's evidence, Mun departed, and the prosecution resumed with its regular witnesses.

Fred Miller implicated all of the defendants in the courtroom and Voss and Svenson, too. He also identified McLean, putting him in *Emerald* in San Francisco and on the boats that met them both in Canada and up at Duxbury Reef. Miller testified that "Me and Harry [Mensing's nickname] didn't know about it [the opium]" until they reached Puget Sound, which helped Mensing's defense.

After George Knight's cross-examination, the government had another dozen witnesses, including *Halcyon*'s builder, William I. Stone, but the case ultimately hinged on the testimony of Smith and Miller. The defense started by aiming at both of them, hoping to damage the two key prosecution witnesses' credibility as much as possible. They also needed the jury to like their clients, calling a series of character witnesses before the first defendant, Louis Greenwald, took the stand.

He denied everything, including ever being in a boat called the *Emerald*, much less smuggling opium. He didn't know Ewen McLean or any of the others and never had anything to do with boats, sailors or the Pacific Ocean. He had gone to Victoria once but had traveled there for "his health" and to look into a gambling investment, nothing to do with opium. His cross-examination took most of the afternoon and resumed on May 16. Greenwald represented a solid link between the *Emerald* ring and the *Halcyon* one before it. The two Knights spent much of Wednesday fighting over how much the jury would be allowed to see of that connection. Sam Knight wanted to impeach Greenwald's testimony with his prior involvement in the *Halcyon*/Whaley conspiracy. George Knight wanted to keep that information out if at all possible. Greenwald didn't help by being vague on as many details as possible and denying anything incriminating, like ties to Chinatown, McLean, Joslyn, Voss or Svenson, but the jury heard about Will Whaley and *Halcyon* all morning.

In many of the other details, Greenwald's memory unfortunately failed him. A newspaper reporter commented sarcastically, "All that Greenewald [*sic*] could not remember about his connection with the ring would make an interesting volume." Greenwald admitted knowing Wichman but denied having any financial relationship with him. Then he admitted that Wichman owed him money and he held an outstanding note for $200 from Wichman. Then it was $250. He said the same for Whaley and then admitted that he'd gone down to Honolulu and met with Whaley, even taking pictures with him and McLean (who he'd earlier said he didn't know) "in Chinese costume." He said he had taken $1,000 that he'd gotten in Victoria and loaned this money to Whaley in Honolulu. Asked if Whaley paid it back, Greenwald said, "No, he never did."

With this, the defense rested. Closing arguments were set for the morning of May 17, and Sam Knight led off for the United States. Once again, he put *Halcyon* front and center, linking three of the four defendants to the old smuggling ring. The other Knight objected, but the remarks got into the record. In this case, the *Emerald* "had been fitted out at this port and proceeded to Victoria and returned laden with contraband opium and Chinese on two separate occasions," and the government had proved it, Knight said. After all was said and done, it still came down to the statements of A.J. Smith and Fred Miller.

That's what George Knight said, too, summing up for the defense before a standing-room-only crowd in the courtroom. He blamed the absent smugglers, McLean, Svenson and Voss, as well as the lying Miller as the "real" conspirators in the case. He showed how none of the defendants profited from the scheme while others had and how Miller had shown a "willingness to lie." His summation took up most of the day, and observers agreed that it was one of the best and most eloquent ever heard in the Northern District of California. Charles A. Garter would get the final word the next morning.

On Friday, May 18, 1894, the *Emerald* and to some degree the *Halcyon* opium rings both drew to a close in federal court in San Francisco. U.S. Attorney Garter made the final summation for the government, and Judge Morrow charged the jury, which retired at 4:05 p.m. to consider the evidence. The three charges left in the indictment were conspiracy, smuggling opium and smuggling aliens. Each carried a two-year penalty. For the conspiracy count, the jurors needed to find that there had been an agreement between two or more people and that one of them had committed some overt act in furtherance of the agreement. The defense, smiling and filled with confidence, watched the jury leave the courtroom, expecting to see them back shortly. At 10:30 p.m., the jury returned, saying they were unable to come to a verdict and some of them thought they never could agree. Judge Morrow sent them back to consider some more, saying the matter was too important to give up so soon and he'd see them in the morning.

The jury had different news on Saturday at 9:30 a.m. "We the jury find Louis Greenwald, George Wichman, George N. Thomas, the prisoners at the bar, guilty as charged, and recommend them to the mercy of the court." The three named were stunned and "despairing," expecting an acquittal or a hung jury at the worst. Charles Mensing, on the other hand, started chuckling even before the clerk read the second slip of paper acquitting him. He walked out of the courtroom a free man. Judge Morrow ordered the three convicts into custody. Thomas took it badly, moaning about his photography business and fainting in the hallway, a deputy marshal catching him as he fell. Marshals transported them to the Alameda County Jail to await sentencing as their lawyers planned appeals. The *Emerald* ring had finally shattered, but now the sharp-edged pieces endangered each other as the co-conspirators negotiated with the government—cooperation in exchange for leniency. Before cutting any more deals, Sam Knight and Charles Garter decided to wait and see what Judge Morrow had in store.

On June 5, they found out. Judge Morrow handed down the maximum possible sentence, two years in prison on each count and a $6,000 fine. Those counts would run consecutively for a total of six years each. He was sending a message, one that countless other judges would repeat over the next 120 years of America's war on drugs: "This condition of affairs is a shame and disgrace, and the time has come when the law must be executed. This Court would not be doing its duty if it did not call attention to this matter at this time, and would not be doing its duty if it failed to properly punish such violations." The prisoners slumped dejectedly as their families collapsed in tears, and their lawyers were "shocked, speechless for several minutes." They finally came to and asked for a stay in sentencing while they appealed, but Judge Morrow was having none of that.

Back to Alameda County the new convicts went, and three days later, the marshals transported them across the bay to their new home for six years, the state prison at San Quentin. There would be some more maneuvering

Louis Greenwald and his two co-conspirators from the *Halcyon* and *Emerald* rings all went to California's San Quentin prison to serve their six-year terms. *California State Library.*

over the next four years, Greenwald in particular trying everything he could to get out of prison, asking for presidential pardons, begging for clemency and, above all, offering repeatedly and very publicly to help with the prosecution of those uncaught. But with the talkative Greenwald, Wichman and Thomas locked up at San Quentin and clamoring to join A.J. Smith on the witness stand, Ewen McLean, C.S. Joslyn and Will Whaley stayed out of the United States and out of reach. They could still stick their fingers in other pies, though. There were just as many smokers out there as before and lots of money to be made in the opium racket, even if a backstabbing partner stole it all. California's Chinatowns might be off limits for McLean and Joslyn, but they still had Hawaii. One thing was for sure: Greenwald, Thomas and Wichman wouldn't be going along this time.

22

OLD FINGERS, NEW RINGS

Halcyon showed everybody what was possible. *Emerald* showed them that *Halcyon* wasn't just a fluke. If you had a ship and some opium, you could get rich, assuming your partner didn't rip you off and your investor didn't snitch to the Treasury Department. Aside from those bad news scenarios, the market outlook appeared excellent for opium futures in 1893, and a fleet of schooners was soon in commission to service that market. The ships were cheap and readily available. Idle schooners lined Victoria's waterfront during the months when the sealers weren't out killing, and there were other vessels in the coasting trade, coming and going from Alaskan, Canadian or American West Coast ports.

Suddenly, however, someone slammed on the brakes. The U.S. Congress, in a rare moment of sensibility, opted to lower the duty on smoking opium to $6, sucking almost all of the profit out of smuggling the drug. The Victoria newspapers described the impact on the opium importers and refiners in town: "The passage yesterday of the new amended tariff bill had its immediate effect in this city of closing down all the large opium factories which for years have done business here…contributing in the neighborhood of $200,000 annually in revenue." With the import duty in Canada at $5 per pound and America's at $6, it once more made sense for the San Francisco firms to openly import direct from Hong Kong. The impact showed up in British Columbia, which recorded imports of almost 29,000 pounds of opium in 1893 and only 7,301 in 1895. The Chinese in America still had to dodge that treaty prohibiting them from importing opium themselves, but they got around that with middlemen, and almost overnight, an era ended. (Until Congress went back to normal and raised the duty again.)

The smugglers weren't totally discouraged. After all, there was still Hawaii. McLean had some experience in that line and had ships on the way. The first ship out of the blocks, however, wasn't Canadian or American or one of the sleek, fast, off-duty sealers. It was a rather tired, fairly old Hawaiian-registered sixty-nine-ton schooner with the mundane name of *Norma*, and Ewen McLean picked it up on the cheap. *Norma*'s ownership was a little cloudy. Officially, it belonged to Frederick D. Walker of Honolulu, a sea captain who had been sailing in the islands and around the Pacific for decades. Walker had taken it to Victoria with a cargo of coconuts and left it there, where he said it'd been chartered by a Canadian fish merchant. Frederick J. Claxton seemed to be a legitimate businessman and made arrangements to use *Norma* to ship four hundred barrels of dried salmon to Honolulu, and if the deal worked out, he said he might make a regular thing of it. Claxton planned to travel along as a passenger to check out Hawaii and the market for fish in the islands.

That was the official story. Behind the scenes, even as the *Emerald* trial was wrapping up in San Francisco in mid-1894, Ewen McLean was making plans for another run down to Honolulu using *Norma*, and he brought some of the *Halcyon* band back to bring it off. He needed a captain, and thanks to the *Emerald* case, he had one. He'd made up with August W. Svenson, who owed McLean for helping Voss rip off the *Emerald* opium. The Swedish bail-jumper didn't have a ship, and he'd already proved he didn't have any scruples about smuggling opium, so that solved one personnel problem. Once again, McLean filled up the crew berths with a couple of old *Halcyon* hands, signing up "Me and Bill." Mate Jim Harvey and seaman Bill Johnson had proved repeatedly that they didn't have any qualms about running opium either, so they were, quite literally, on board.

Like McLean, Svenson was still a fugitive, wanted in the United States, but McLean had no plans for *Norma* to go into American waters. In October 1894, the schooner headed up to Claxton's processing plant on the Skeena River to collect the salmon. Somewhere along the way, they loaded two to six thousand pounds of opium aboard. They had to hide the tins, probably in with the fish. *Norma* had none of *Halcyon*'s speed, and if challenged, it'd have to stop, submit to a search and hope for the best.

Once again, thanks to spies and snitches, the Hawaiians had a pretty good idea that the *Norma* was on the way and bringing bad news with it. The informers told the customs men and the Hawaiian consul, and the newspapers picked up the rumors, which Walker, in Honolulu, denied. Claxton's presence was difficult to explain; he appeared to be legitimate, with no reason to take all of the risks associated with smuggling opium. Was he a dupe, unknowingly providing cover for the opium ring's scheme? We can't know for certain 120 years later, but it seems odd that a wealthy executive would subject himself to the discomforts and dangers of a winter voyage on the North Pacific in a fairly small sailing vessel when he could have gotten to Honolulu as McLean did in the first-class cabin of a Canadian Mail steam ship.

After leaving British Columbia in the first week in November, the schooner finally put into Honolulu on February 1, 1895, a three-month passage, which normally took even a slow sailer like *Norma* thirty days or less. The ship was expected in mid-December, and when it arrived, the customs men brought *Norma* into port and gave it a thorough inspection, finding nothing but the four hundred barrels of salmon declared on the papers. Captain Svenson sailed back to Victoria as a passenger on the SS *Miowera*, and in April, Claxton told the Honolulu papers that he still hadn't sold all of his salmon and he was "discouraged by the whole business." The dejected Claxton finally left Honolulu on May 3, and he apparently had enough of the *Norma*. The fish magnate went back to British Columbia in style, traveling first class on the *Miowera*. Having served its purpose, *Norma* was left at the pier in Honolulu, eventually getting a new owner and new captain and going into the interisland trade.

But what of the opium? J.E. Lawton, who claimed to be one of the crewmen, peddling his story to the newspapers in 1901, said that *Norma* brought six thousand pounds, carrying it directly into Honolulu Harbor and dropping it overboard, where it was recovered later by divers. It was a thrilling tale, with lots of details, but almost none of it was true, and the parts that were, Lawton could have gotten by reading the same newspapers everyone else did. He did, however, point the finger at one man whose role in the scheme was indisputable because he cheerfully admitted it, then and later.

Patrick "Paddy" Curtis was born in Ireland and immigrated to the United States as a boy. He joined the Union army at the beginning of the Civil War, serving briefly in the Sixth New York Cavalry Regiment before deserting. After a decent interval, Curtis joined the Union navy, where he finished out the conflict. When the war ended, he stayed a sailor, eventually drifting into Honolulu, where he became a fisherman and a local character. Curtis was the proud owner of a fine little sailboat, the sloop *Spray*, built, coincidentally, by William I. Stone, the same man who put *Halcyon* on San Francisco Bay.

Spray. Patrick "Paddy" Curtis's little cutter carried *Norma*'s opium from Lanai to Honolulu. *Bancroft Library, University of California, Berkeley.*

Spray came to Hawaii and fell into Curtis's hands. It was just big enough to make interisland trips in some safety but not so big that it could profitably haul any cargoes unless they were very high-value items—like opium. Curtis was a lot like Will Whaley in that he didn't much care who knew what he and *Spray* were up to, and he cared even less after he'd had a couple of drinks, so he didn't hide the fact that he was taking *Spray* out toward Lanai in May 1895. He admitted years later that he'd gone to pick up the opium cached by the *Norma* crew at Manele Bay—the same spot where *Halcyon* had dropped a big part of its cargo of Lai Yuen in 1891. Curtis successfully retrieved the buried tins and brought them back to Honolulu's buyers, but he wasn't the first to try to recover the load. Two others had gone before him in March. Their trip, though, had an unhappy ending.

While *Norma* idled at the dock in Honolulu, two of the crew, "Me and Bill," the old team of Jim Harvey and Bill Johnson, set out with a local Portuguese fisherman identified only as "Tom." The trio took a sailboat even smaller than *Spray* off to the southeast, toward the Neighbor Islands of Molokai and Lanai. Fragments of the boat were found later on shore, but "Me and Bill" and their companion were gone. They had survived the wreck of the *Halcyon*, but they'd taken their chances one too many times, and smuggler's luck had finally run out.

Smuggler's luck ran both ways for another of the opium ring's members in 1894. On July 24, the SS *Warrimoo* arrived in Honolulu from Vancouver, bringing with it a Colonel Fred Jamieson of Vancouver and his assorted baggage. This included four large trunks, which went into the custom house for inspection. All four were found to contain opium, about $6,000 worth. The inspectors closed up the trunks and waited for Colonel Jamieson to make an appearance and collect his property. By the end of the day, the trunks had gone uncalled for, and the police were sent out to look for Jamieson, starting in the local hotels.

The detectives quickly discovered that nobody by the name of Jamieson had checked into the Honolulu hotels. However, at the Arlington, just up Bishop Street from the steamer pier, a *Warrimoo* passenger from Medicine Hat, Northwest Territory, had signed in. The name on the register was C.S. Joslyn. And the detectives noticed something odd about Mr. Joslyn, besides the fact that he matched the description of Fred Jamieson to a T. Nobody named Joslyn was listed on the *Warrimoo*'s passenger manifest.

By the following morning, the detectives had decided they needed to speak with Mr. Joslyn, but he was nowhere to be found. The *Warrimoo* sailed that afternoon for Victoria and Vancouver, and Joslyn was safely aboard, as the chagrined local officials later discovered. The Hawaiian government said that Joslyn would be prosecuted if he showed up again, and to top it off, they asked the United States to forward its warrant from the *Emerald* case down to the islands. If C.S. Joslyn came back, he'd spend some time in Oahu Prison and then Hawaii would ship him to San Francisco for the Americans to try. And those same officials took note of the fact that another *Emerald* fugitive had recently been in town. They asked the Americans to send that other warrant down to Honolulu too. This one was for Ewen W. McLean. At the beginning of 1895, Hawaii had barred the door and said farewell to at least two members of the opium ring, but they hadn't heard the last from C.S. Joslyn or Ewen McLean, not by a long shot. In fact, the two smugglers were about to humiliate Hawaii in a most public fashion.

Joslyn's name would come up again soon and McLean's, too, because the two of them had been scheming on more than just the *Norma*'s load and four trunks during their time in Hawaii. On November 7, 1895, the schooner *Henrietta* sailed from Victoria for La Paz, Mexico. On December 21, it turned up at Kea`au, Hawaii, 2,500 miles off course. As the schooner anchored off the coast, C.E. Gale, one of the crewmen, came ashore, supposedly looking for water for his ship, and ran into a constable, who called his boss, the deputy sheriff for Waianae. Smuggler's luck turned extremely bad at this moment, because the deputy sheriff in these parts now was our old friend Billy Sheldon.

The deputy, hearing that a strange schooner was hovering off Waianae and had just set a man on the beach, put two and two together and got exactly opium. He immediately arrested Gale and then went hunting for the ship. First, he called customs and got a tugboat with some help to come out from Honolulu. The customs officers located *Henrietta*, boarded it and found out that it was in Hawaiian waters from a foreign port. This made the ship subject to inspection. The search turned up 1,400 pounds of opium. They arrested everyone on board and towed *Henrietta* triumphantly into Honolulu Harbor.

As obsessed as ever, Billy Sheldon's very first question to his suspects was, "Is Lycurgus aboard?" It's a good thing for George Lycurgus that he wasn't, but the haul was satisfactory enough, with Gale, Captain William B. Anderson, mate Herbert "Bert" Wheeler, seamen J.H. Brown and Michael Connell and ship's cook Ho Wai all locked up at the Honolulu Jail, along with the opium.

Here, though, the officers got their first unpleasant shock of the day. As they examined the 3,740 five-*tael* tins, they noticed something unusual. They all looked rather familiar. In fact, the officers realized with a sinking feeling that they had seen these tins once before—and seized them once before. Almost every tin bore the stamp of the Hawaiian Customs Service. Ewen McLean had pulled this scam back in 1885, buying seized Hawaiian opium at a government auction and taking it to the mainland, but even he hadn't been cheeky enough to turn around and smuggle it straight back into the islands. Surely, nobody had that much chutzpah. Well, this time, it appeared that somebody did. The buyer of the opium at the auction the Hawaiian government had arranged back in March was none other than C.S. Joslyn. And the owner of record of the *Henrietta* was Thomas Flewin, a furrier and merchant, but that was just a front. The true owner was Ewen W. McLean.

Joslyn and McLean were safe in Victoria—out of reach and not coming anywhere near Hawaii anytime soon. The embarrassed Hawaiians did have somebody handy to take their frustration out on and did so, unloading on the crew of the *Henrietta*. A trial and appeals to Hawaii's Supreme Court followed the arrest, but the end result was imprisonment "at hard labor" on the Reef for Captain Anderson and his crew. Their defense, that they didn't know that there was opium aboard, was destroyed by testimony that the crew removed it from containers and repackaged it aboard the schooner while en route. By April 1896, they were on the Reef, and armed guards watched over the entire crew as it made small rocks out of big ones in a local quarry, even the "gentleman" Gale taking to the work "like a little man."

Mate Wheeler, the two seamen and Ho Wai, the cook, were released in May 1897 and shipped back to Canada. Gale was freed that December, and Anderson won a pardon in January 1898 after providing a complete account of the entire operation (and blaming Gale for most of it). And Gale happened to be the right person to blame, because he was more than just a passenger for *Henrietta*'s trip to Waianae, and his name wasn't Gale. It was George D. Wade, and he was a well-known opium smuggler from Victoria, British Columbia, and Portland, Oregon. Not only that, but he'd also been acquainted with prison accommodations before. Wade was arrested and convicted for smuggling in 1892 and again in 1894, about the time that the *Emerald* ring defendants were getting sentenced to San Quentin. The federal judge in Seattle sent Wade to the relatively new United States penitentiary on McNeil Island, Washington, to do his two years at hard labor.

Prison life must have disagreed with Wade, who escaped with another opium smuggler, John Brooks, on September 27, 1894, only two months after the two had been locked up together. Although Brooks would be recaptured, Wade made it to Victoria, and his adventures to Hawaii began with McLean and Joslyn. Returned by Hawaii to Canada in December 1897, he stayed in British Columbia until the heat died down and then drifted north to the Alaskan gold fields, where he was busted in Nome for stealing gold from other people's sluices. This got Wade sent right back to McNeil Island, which he didn't like any more than he had the first time he was there. On July 4, 1905 (Independence Day, appropriately enough), Wade and seven other inmates broke out of the prison and vanished. Police recaptured the seven, but George Wade, the leader of the escape, was never seen or heard from again.

George Wade, also known as C.E. Gale. McLean's man aboard the schooner *Henrietta*, seized by Billy Sheldon at Waianae, Hawaii, in 1895. *National Archives.*

Thus ends the saga of the schooner *Henrietta*, except for the fate of the 3,740 tins of reseized opium. Having already seized it twice, the abashed authorities in Honolulu wisely decided not to sell the *Henrietta*'s cargo at auction this time. Instead, they rented a tugboat and a barge, loaded the latter with all that opium and towed it out to sea. At a suitable distance offshore, a team of workers set to breaking open tins and dumping the contents behind the barge. Soon a muddy brown slick trailed out behind them, a fleeting and sorry reminder of smuggler's bad luck.

The *Henrietta* run had been a failure, costing the ring 1,400 pounds of opium and a ship, but they didn't discourage easily. In fact, McLean and Joslyn were a lot more sanguine about opium futures in Hawaii than the customs officers in the Islands. Why? Because the government hadn't auctioned off 1,400 pounds of opium in Victoria in March 1895. They auctioned off *10,000* pounds. This netted the Hawaiian government $50,000, but simple arithmetic said that 8,600 pounds was still out there somewhere and in the hands of men who fully intended to smuggle it back into the Hawaiian Islands from whence it had come.

The year 1896 passed quietly, sliding by without a major seizure but with plenty of small ones by the police in Honolulu. This meant that the opium was still coming, and the spies employed by deputy collector Frank B. McStocker told him that the ring managed a successful run that year using a schooner whose name is lost to history. That got them into 1897, and Ewen McLean was taking a much more conservative line on these projects. McLean now had a family with three boys and two girls, and with Hawaii and the United States both off-limits, he was spending a lot more time at home, doing the organizing and planning. Others were still getting their hands dirty, however.

On June 9, 1897, the little schooner *Lena L* sailed from Port Townsend, Washington, supposedly in ballast, down the coast for Guaymas, Mexico. It was a petite ship, only fifty feet long and twenty-nine tons, with a crew of four and one passenger. The captain, Charles Prellberg, was petite too. At four foot five, he didn't take up much room on the little schooner. The passenger wasn't much bigger, and he wasn't in great health. Halfway through the voyage, Prellberg reported, his passenger asked to be taken to the nearest port. Due to a navigation error or some other mix-up, the pint-sized Prellberg took them all the way to Honolulu, 2,400 miles off course, arriving forty-two days after leaving Port Townsend. Amazingly, his passenger immediately felt much better. Maybe the sea air was good for the tubercular lungs of Albert Weinrich Wilson after all.

The Hawaiian authorities were not buying Prellberg's fairy tale, but a close inspection of the *Lena L* turned up not an ounce of opium. There had been several reports of the schooner hovering offshore several days before at Waianae again, near *Halcyon*'s old offload site and the same beaches where *Henrietta* came to grief. It appeared that the *Lena L* had been in the neighborhood for at least a week before it finally "put her nose into the harbor," but nobody could prove it landed anything. Wilson, who was using the name "Weinrich" on this trip, checked into a local hotel while Prellberg sold the *Lena L* to a customs officer and a harbor policeman. They got a bargain, as the former owners were anxious to be gone. Three days after they arrived, Weinrich, Prellberg and the entire crew boarded the SS *Miowera* and sailed for Victoria, mission accomplished.

The year 1898 brought the swan song for the ring, as the members began to age, die and retire from the business. McLean, living full time in Victoria, raising a family and working as a Chinese translator, got a commission as a notary public, trying to get some legitimate business ventures going with the proceeds of his smuggling operations. Joslyn, still under indictment down south, worked something out with the federal government, because he was able to travel back to San Francisco, at least to visit. Albert Wilson, whose tuberculosis was about to kill him, took one last ocean voyage, this one aboard the schooner *Labrador*, which cleared Victoria on April 23, supposedly for a sealing cruise off Japan.

In another of those weird, drastic navigational errors that seemed to plague only opium runners, *Labrador* fetched up on Maui on June 25, with Albert Wilson a very sick man. Recognizing Wilson, having heard this song before and very suspicious after the whole *Lena L* episode, customs thought *Labrador* was a smuggler, too, but like the *Lena L*, the latest arrival was clean. Captain John Haake said that he'd been headed for the Bonins when his seaman, Wilson, fell sick. Mentally disturbed by his illness, Wilson assaulted Haake, who displayed a cut and some bruises to prove it and said he'd had to handcuff Wilson, who he planned to put ashore on Maui to get rid of him. Haake and his mate, Joseph Carter, both denied knowing anything about any opium. Of course, Wilson did too.

The customs men took everybody ashore on Maui and then separated Haake, Carter and Wilson from the cook, getting a Japanese-speaking officer from Honolulu to go to work on him. Offered immunity from prosecution and $500, the cook spilled the beans, saying he'd show the officers where the opium had been hidden. Sure enough, there was one thousand pounds buried on the beach on the island of Kahoolawe, across a short channel from Maui. The smugglers had marked the cache with one of *Labrador*'s anchors, which the happy customs men had already noticed was missing from the schooner.

With the opium in hand, the police arrested Haake, Carter and Wilson, who was attempting to pretend that he was not the Albert Weinrich who had previously visited Hawaii aboard the *Lena L.* Nobody believed that, but everyone could see that the little German lunger really was sick. His case of tuberculosis already well advanced, he spent some nights in Honolulu coughing up blood in the city jail before everyone agreed he'd be better off in the hospital. The sheriff neglected to put a guard on Wilson, who looked too sick to move. Wilson might have been sick, but he wasn't stupid, and he wasn't that sick, either. He shaved off his beard, walked about five blocks to the steamer pier and boarded the SS *Warrimoo* as it was about to sail for Victoria. By the time the authorities in Honolulu figured out that his hospital bed was empty, Albert Weinrich Wilson was out of Hawaiian waters and not planning to go back. Most people guessed (correctly) that he'd be dead soon anyway and turned their attention to the two people and the ship they did still have in custody.

They almost lost the ship. Before it could be moved from its anchorage on Maui, a gale came up and threw *Labrador*, minus its bigger anchor, ashore at Makena Beach. Dismasted and with a hole in its bow, the ship could be repaired, but this was another embarrassment for customs chief Frank McStocker and his men. McStocker made up for the disappointments by seeing that Haake and Carter were prosecuted to the fullest extent of the law. Both men were convicted and given substantial prison terms at hard labor. Two years later, both were still on the Reef when the census man came to do his count. The government forfeited *Labrador* and sold it at auction. It went into the interisland trade under a new owner. Although they tried, the customs men were unable to charge the buyer of the load, an old familiar face in the opium business. Sun Ah Mi, prominent Maui businessman, had previously bid for Kalākaua's last opium license and partnered with winner

WHERE THE SCHOONER LABRADOR LIES.

Schooner *Labrador* ashore at Maui, Hawaii, in 1898. Pacific Commercial Advertiser, *June 17, 1898.*

Chun Lung. Sun's luck held, but smuggler's luck had turned disastrous for the rest of the ring on this, the last of their opium runs.

Labrador did represent a final hurrah. In 1898, the United States annexed Hawaii, putting it off-limits for McLean, Joslyn, Voss and Svenson. (Although Svenson got his charges dismissed on grounds that his health was "ruined," and he couldn't stand trial.) But the thing they'd started was too big to stop. More smugglers were already on the water—more ships and new rings. "Opium Brown," the nickname of one mysterious smuggler who came and went from Hawaii as Whaley had, followed the *Halcyon* ring's playbook like he had an autographed copy. Brown (whose real name was Billy Stewart) gave way to a second Opium Brown, known in the newspapers and by the police as "Opium Brown Number 2." Both of these men were smuggling loads into Hawaii well after 1900, and they weren't the only ones. Smuggling schooners like the *Retriever*, the *South Bend* and unknown ships came and went without leaving their names behind. These served Opium Brown and other smugglers until Canada banned smoking opium in 1908. The prohibition shut down the Victoria factories for good after a thirty-year run.

America wasn't far behind. In the months leading up to the first International Opium Conference in Shanghai in 1909, the United States passed its own ban. On February 9, the Opium Exclusion Act of 1909 prohibited the importation of opium for smoking (but not the kind that went into patent and proprietary medicines; that was still fine). The two statutes, Canada's and the United States', changed the face of the drug traffic. After 1909, the use of purpose-built ships like *Halcyon* to carry opium withered away. Because the opium could no longer be purchased openly in Victoria, the 750-mile run to San Francisco and the 2,500-mile run to Honolulu suddenly turned into a 9,000-mile round trip to Hong Kong. Whaley had done it, Billy Stewart followed suit several years later with his own ship, *Retriever*, and others followed him, but pulling this off on a regular basis was just not practical. It took too long, cost too much and the risks—*Halcyon* was wrecked in a typhoon, for example, and *Retriever* lost a mast in a storm and was attacked by Filipino rebels—too many. After 1909, the smugglers all went back to concealing their shipments in the growing merchant commerce between Asia and the United States. And in Hawaii, now a part of the United States, nobody inspected ships coming from San Francisco, Los Angeles or Seattle any longer. Smugglers didn't even have to try very hard on those vessels. The United States Customs Service at Honolulu only checked the ones arriving from Canada and Asia.

The opium still poured in, of course. No law, even one boldly and hopefully called the Opium Exclusion Act, was going to stop that flow. America still had a large number of people—Chinese and others—who wanted to smoke the drug and were willing to pay to get it. Stopping the traffic now was out of the question. As the saying goes, that ship had sailed long ago. Funnily enough, we know the ship's name and when it sailed. The date was August 10, 1887, and the ship, of course, was *Halcyon*.

23

DEATH SHALL COME TO YOU FROM THE SEA

Master Mariner Alfred B. Metcalf's odyssey carried him to the far corners of the world—to the land of the lotus-eaters in Hong Kong, the rocky shores of Japan and the sea cliffs of Hawaii. He'd been hunted by the revenue men of three countries and spent years treating every strange sail and every puff of smoke on an endless, empty horizon as an enemy. In 1895, Metcalf, now sixty-two years old and with a liver considerably older than that, finally turned his back on the sea. He didn't put an oar on his shoulder that day, and he didn't walk as Odysseus did on his trek inland from the harbor, but Metcalf didn't go far before he found people who didn't care about oars or ships or broken-down old sea captains. He barely made it past downtown Los Angeles.

Metcalf's wanderings included a lost half decade following *Halcyon*'s trip back from Hawaii. Where he went and what he did in those years, 1891 to 1895, are a mystery. He never returned to San Francisco, where a wife, two daughters and seven grandchildren might normally have warmed an old sailor's retirement from the sea. Eventually, he turned up. In 1895, the railroads were paying people to go to Los Angeles; land was dirt cheap, and the population was swelling in the city and the suburbs that popped up around it. Metcalf settled first in what is now the Boyle Heights area just east of downtown Los Angeles, and even in 1895, this wasn't the nicest neighborhood in the city. In fact, Metcalf's rooming house sat on Anderson Street, a hardscrabble road mere feet from the railroad tracks (and on the "wrong" side of them). His little room was close by the Los Angeles River flowing sluggishly nearby. A hundred years later, workers digging a subway line discovered opium pipe bowls under Boyle Heights, along with the bones of Chinese men buried there in a potter's field.

Within a year, Metcalf moved to a more upscale neighborhood at the foot of the Hollywood Hills that was the home of his younger brother, Henry. Here he stayed for the years left to him. It was here that he died. The obituary, printed in the Los Angeles papers on September 9, 1903, is straightforward enough. "Captain Alfred B. Metcalf, aged 70, funeral private." It's the sparse word of the lonely passing of a man whose death came from the sea, that of a captain who went down with his ship, and in the account of the wreck there is no report of any survivors. Whoever sent the notice to the paper included his title, but Metcalf himself had no more pretensions. In the last census that counted him, he gave the taker no occupation at all, and in his last city directory entry, Alfred Metcalf, no longer the "sea captain" or "master mariner" he had once so proudly proclaimed, described himself simply as a "sailor."

Albert Weinrich Wilson, the man who bought *Halcyon* from Grant and Morrow and helped finance the early runs, faded quickly after his narrow 1898 escape from Hawaii. His tuberculosis was well advanced by the time he got back to Victoria on the SS *Warrimoo*. The Hawaiian authorities, frustrated at losing the key man in the *Labrador*'s capture, took it out on the rest of the schooner's crew, nailing the two men they still had, Captain John Haake and his mate, Joe Carter, with five-year terms on the Reef. That was what A.W. Wilson should have gotten and would have if he hadn't slipped out of the hospital and stowed away in the nick of time. But Judge TB had a harsher sentence for the little German, who faced winter coming on in Canada with no ability to go south to warmer climes now that Hawaii, where warrants were outstanding, was part of the United States, and the marshals would be waiting. A prisoner of the bacillus, Wilson swilled his opium-laced patent medicines and waited in the cold for the end to come.

It came on February 28, 1899. He was only thirty-five years old, buried in the Ross Bay Cemetery at the edge of the water in Victoria, a lonely end in a foreign graveyard. There was no notice of the death in the Victoria papers, no reason for any publicity, nothing notable about the passing. Like Metcalf's notice, Wilson's death certificate listed no survivors, and like Metcalf, his occupation was given as "sailor."

Charles Sumner Joslyn, ship's purser, capitalist and Prince of Smugglers, finally left the sea and the opium business behind him. Under indictment in San Francisco for the *Emerald* ring case, he stayed out of reach in Victoria until that threat finally passed, which would have been about the same date that Louis Greenwald, George Wichman and George N. Thomas walked free out of the gate at San Quentin. Before that day, they'd made it abundantly clear in every way possible that they would simply love to testify against Joslyn, McLean, Voss and anybody else the feds asked them about. After that release date, the three, with no more motive to snitch, became much less of a threat.

Joslyn returned with his wife, Elise, to San Francisco in 1900, moving into a new house at 822 Alvarado Street in the Noe Valley section of the city. He was sixty-one, and aside from a few fishing expeditions down to Monterey or up to Napa, he stayed close to home, those long ocean voyages a thing of his past. Elise passed in May 1903, and Joslyn died in Napa, California, on December 13 the same year. He was buried at the IOOF cemetery in San Francisco.

The thoroughly rotten **John C. Voss** fled to Victoria ahead of the *Emerald* ring indictment, taking the money he'd stolen and using it to go into the hotel and saloon business. He did well for several years, possibly because the captain, who still had no moral scruples whatsoever, augmented his income by shanghaiing unwary sailors who came in for a drink, using the knockout drops the crimps of San Francisco found so effective back in the 1880s.

In 1901, mostly on a bet, he partnered with a journalist to try an around-the-world voyage in a small boat. He found a Native canoe, a dugout carved from a cedar log, purchased it (shamelessly boasting that he got a substantial discount by liquoring up the Native Canadian owner first) and settled in to make some modifications. The captain, who was the only real sailor in the two-man crew, added three stubby masts and a small cabin, and the *Tilikum* ("Friend") set sail in 1901.

Voss, still wanted in the *Emerald* case, took some precautions to avoid any unpleasant encounters with a United States marshal. He registered *Tilikum* under a new name, *Pelican*; was careful to avoid the West Coast and Hawaii, where a warrant for his arrest was outstanding; and steered clear of the American revenue cutters.

After forty thousand miles, many adventures, eleven different mates (one of whom he allegedly murdered in a drunken rage and another who locked him in the cabin at gunpoint until he sobered up) and three years, three months and twelve days, he reached England, where he gave up the attempt to circumnavigate. He returned to Canada, took on some sea captain jobs, became a sealer in Japan for several years and finally retired to Tracy, California, after the indictment had been forgotten. There he drove a jitney cab until he died in 1922.

John Voss and *Tilikum*, the dugout canoe he sailed for forty thousand miles from Victoria to England. He carefully avoided the United States. The Venturesome Voyages of Captain Voss.

Before going, though, he wrote an account of his travels, *The Venturesome Voyages of Captain Voss*, which was published in his lifetime and is still in print as *40,000 Miles in a Canoe*, a remarkably good, if self-serving, memoir that naturally never mentions his earlier role as an opium and alien smuggler (and cargo hijacker). *Tilikum*, restored, is now housed at the Maritime Museum of British Columbia in Victoria.

Albion J. "A.J." Smith held onto his gig as a special agent with the U.S. Treasury Department for a few months after the *Emerald* case verdicts came down, doing detective work and hunting for alien and opium smugglers. He was in it for the money, looking for rewards from the feds and establishing a furious correspondence with the San Francisco consul of the Hawaiian Republic, trying to feed them information about George Lycurgus and the Greeks. Unfortunately for Smith, all of the people in the smuggling business and everybody else in California had heard about his testimony in the *Emerald* case, so nobody trusted him anymore. Cut off from any inside knowledge or access and with no real investigative skill, he floundered, and the Treasury Department turned him loose.

So did the Hawaiians, who figured out an easier way to deal with Lycurgus and the Camarinos brothers—putting them on ships bound for California and getting them out of their hair. An unemployed Smith, married with two children, had already lost his freight clerk job, and prospects were grim. With the reward money from the *Emerald* case, he opened a saloon and bought a boardinghouse, operating these for the next few years as the century turned. He supported the little family on the boardinghouse income and by working at odd jobs until the years before World War I, when he got more stable employment, joining the U.S. Customs Service again, this time as a guard.

Smith spent his remaining years in the Customs Service, taking time off during the war, when he enlisted in the navy, serving as a lieutenant, junior grade. After the war, he returned to customs, working as a guard and earning his mate and master mariner licenses. Smith, like so many others in the *Halcyon* ring, had become a sailor, though he kept close to home. He died in 1928 and is buried with his wife, Catharina, at the national cemetery at the Presidio in San Francisco.

Thomas E. Evans became an immigration agent and moved to Hong Kong to obtain contract laborers for Hawaii's sugar planters. After the United States annexed Hawaii in 1898, contract labor and Chinese immigration both became more complicated, if not outright illegal, under the American law that now governed the islands. Evans, who had been running a couple of other shady schemes in Hong Kong, gave up on aliens and moved to Manila, joining with his old pal Will Whaley in a theater venture. Tommy had his fingers in some other pies, including a saloon and some procurement contracts for the U.S. military. This turned sour, and the government investigated Evans for fraud in a case that eventually fell through the cracks as Evans moved on. After his failed attempt to marry a rich young widow, he returned to Hawaii, where in 1903 he died on Maui at age fifty-five.

Demetrius Camarinos, the key man on the receiving end of the Halcyon ring, was up to his neck in the counterrevolution that hoped to restore Liliʻuokalani to her lost throne in 1895. When that fell apart in less than a week, the conspirators, including brother Peter, were rounded up and marched down to the Reef to be tried for treason, a hanging offense. Demetrius avoided all of this commotion by being in San Francisco at the time and lobbied hard with the Greek embassy in Washington to get help for Peter and their fellow countrymen locked up in Honolulu. His pressure might have contributed to the Provisional Government's decision to exile rather than hang the Greeks and the other counterrevolutionaries, and Demetrius was waiting on the pier in San Francisco when Peter got off the RMSS *Arawa* in March.

Neither one of them stayed away forever, and Demetrius eventually returned to the islands to stay, and he continued to be successful in business. He opened an ice cream parlor in downtown Honolulu on the site of the old California Fruit Market in 1901 and a saloon for anyone who wanted something a little harder. One of the pioneers in Hawaii's pineapple industry, he got back in that business and started another pineapple and banana plantation in Hilo before his death in Honolulu in 1903. He is buried in Oahu Cemetery in Honolulu.

George Lycurgus, the man who couldn't be caught no matter how hard Billy Sheldon tried, outlived everybody. He returned to Hawaii from San Francisco, though he'd been banished for life by the new government, betting that nobody cared anymore. He opened a restaurant downtown, the very popular Union Grill, where he hosted parties for his fellow counterrevolutionaries. He eventually moved to the Big Island of Hawaii, where he bought a hotel property, the Volcano House, which sits on the rim of the active Kilauea Crater. Here, he would be instrumental in creating the Hawaii Volcanoes National Park and would host presidents and kings and commoners for the next five decades, leaving all the others from the opium ring behind. Lycurgus was an unapologetic royalist, loyal to Queen Lili'uokalani to the very end, maintaining a shrine to the deposed queen in the hotel. He freely (some would say boastingly) admitted smuggling liquor and guns for the counterrevolution of 1895, but while people tried to get him to concede it, he never confessed to smuggling opium.

24

FITTING ENDINGS

All good things must come to an end, and the bad ones, too. *Halcyon*'s time was up when it got too famous, and Ewen McLean's was up when he had a U.S. marshal waiting for him almost everywhere he went. The opium ring broke up, pieces rolling off in separate directions, but the business it started carried on full speed ahead. That business is part of all of our lives now; we should know what happened to the two men and the ship who brought it to us.

He was the White boy who spoke Chinese like a native and sold opium and morphine for Crane & Brigham in San Francisco. He played both sides in the customs service and tried to smuggle Hawaiian dope back into Hawaii. He was the boy who quit school at fourteen and got the rest of his education the hard way, smuggling Chinese immigrants and setting up opium rings. That boy finally made it, and boy, when he did, he made it big. Ewen Wainwright McLean went legit at about the time Albert Wilson came back from the islands in late 1898 on the *Warrimoo*, babbling about his close call with the Hawaiian police and customs men. With the *Labrador* seized and its opium locked up in a Honolulu customs vault, McLean finally saw the writing on the wall. Like Wilson, he was only thirty-five that year, still a young man in a young man's game, but he had four children to raise. It was time, he thought, to get out of the old life and get into the new.

McLean still possessed considerable skills; he had the Chinese language and quite a knack for business, although he'd been diligently applying these for more than a decade to schemes on the wrong side of the law. That law limited his options; the *Emerald* ring indictment in San Francisco still hung over his head like a sword. All of the United States was out of bounds for him unless he wanted to join Wichman, Thomas and Greenwald in San Quentin. Sharing prison accommodations with those fellows didn't sound too attractive. It was an easy decision as he and Ella settled down with the boys and a baby daughter in Victoria, where they and another girl to come would grow up Canadian. McLean, after he finally gave up opium for good and began looking for something legitimate, knew he couldn't irritate the Canadian authorities too badly. He was a guest in their country, and it wouldn't take much effort or provocation to ship an American fugitive a few miles south to the border.

Ewen Wainwright McLean. Second king of the opium ring, McLean organized the *Emerald*'s two smuggling runs and Halcyon's last. British Columbia from the Earliest Times to the Present, *Volume 4*.

He started with what he knew and went into Victoria's Chinatown to teach English to those who wanted to learn and to give a hand to those who needed a little coaching on how to cross the border. He hung out a shingle as a Chinese translator and got a notary public commission, helping Chinese businesses navigate the Canadian bureaucracy. McLean helped with the paperwork, getting a good reputation with the Chinese, so much so that when a Chinese mob retaliated against some Canadian exclusionists, one of McLean's influential Chinese friends sent his relatives to McLean's home to be sure that he and his family would be untouched by the violence.

He stayed out of trouble for the most part, but in 1900, the government yanked his notary public commission in connection with what must have seemed an old, familiar song, immigration fraud. McLean and another notary were issuing certificates to Japanese people who claimed to have been in Canada for the year required to obtain citizenship, when in fact most were "fresh off the boat," and McLean, though he denied it, knew or should have known it. The scam upset the Canadians but didn't annoy them enough to ship McLean back to the waiting American Treasury agents. Still, it had been a close call, and McLean decided to move his headquarters out of Victoria to Vancouver before the authorities started asking uncomfortable questions about old immigration fraud cases in San Francisco. Ferdinand Ciprico, sitting in San Quentin prison, could tell them a few things about his old partner in crime and would be happy to do so. McLean packed up the family, now three boys and two girls, and headed for the mainland and greener pastures.

It turned out to be the right move and the start of about ten new careers in the next ten years. In those years, he sold cigars, coal, houses, insurance, loans, horses, stocks, oil and saws—almost everything except drugs, it seems—and he dabbled in other areas, like real estate development, architecture, banking and even bridge construction. Before he knew it, he was the president of the A.J. Burton Saw Company, selling blades to the logging industry, and owner of an oil drilling and exploration outfit and a real estate company that sold house lots all over Vancouver, as well as a couple other enterprises, also successful. Everything he touched, it seemed, turned to gold, and he might have wondered once or twice why he hadn't gone legit years ago. In short order, Ewen W. McLean became a "Vancouver Pioneer," one of the respected men who transformed a nothing little waterfront burg into British Columbia's commercial capital and replaced Victoria as Canada's West Coast hub.

He did make a couple of minor modifications. In Vancouver, McLean changed his name, adding a second *a*, and became MacLean, which probably didn't confuse the American authorities south of the border, but they lost interest as the new century turned and other active opium rings demanded attention. In Vancouver, the "prominent capitalist," as one writer called him, joined with some other investors to found the Vancouver Stock Exchange in 1907, where McLean would be listed as a member and broker for the rest of his life. The exchange is noted today as a source for venture capital and features mining and oil and gas stocks, but for decades after its founding, it was mostly known as a haven for frauds, swindles and confidence games. Nobody today remembers that it was originally bankrolled, along with a number of other legitimate Vancouver businesses, with the proceeds of a decade of opium smuggling and human trafficking. It appears that even in 1907, nobody knew or cared that the straitlaced, clean-cut chap whose picture and biography made it into *Who's Who in Western Canada* was once the biggest smuggler on the West Coast and still a wanted fugitive in another country.

Ewen McLean had arrived. He became a member of Vancouver's prestigious Terminal City Club and the Vancouver Exhibition Association. He owned show horses and watched his daughters ride, and he held shares in the Vancouver Horse Show. Over the years, he served as a director on several boards, including Dominion Trust Company, a major financial institution that survived in Canada until 1993, and the Pacific Marine

Insurance Company, where he sat in meetings with a future lieutenant governor of British Columbia.

In 1909, the U.S. government dismissed the old *Emerald* charges against McLean, Voss, Svenson and *Halcyon*'s last captain, Charles Johnson, and McLean celebrated his success in the way Harry Tevis and other rich men did: buying a yacht, the handsome Seattle cutter *Lavita*. He brought it north to join the fleet at the posh Royal Vancouver Yacht Club, where McLean and his stepson, Charles O. Julian Jr., would race it. Lavita means "the life" in Italian, and one can't help wondering which life—the new one or the old secret one that got him here in the first place—he was celebrating.

McLean retired from business in 1919. The other ventures, boards and directorships provided an adequate income without a lot of effort; certainly, there was no longer any need to wait anxiously for word of a schooner days overdue delivering its cargo to a remote beach and customers demanding their product. He and Ella took a vacation in 1919 and 1920, boarding the SS *Empress of Asia* on Christmas Day 1919, the Canadian Pacific Mail liner bound for Honolulu, Yokohama and Hong Kong, one last transpacific journey.

This time, Ewen McLean returned to his childhood home as a tourist. The world had changed in the forty years since young Ewen McLean left St. Paul's College as a boy. In 1909, the American government banned the importation of smoking opium altogether. Canada prohibited the traffic in smoking opium a few months earlier in 1908, both countries getting in line with world opinion that would be expressed at the International Opium Commission meeting in Shanghai in 1909. No longer were seized five-tael tins of Lai Yuen opium auctioned off on the courthouse steps in San Francisco. No more schooners loaded up in Victoria for the run down the coast to Drake's Bay or Monterey. Those days were long gone, and by 1919, they were mostly forgotten. People were still smuggling, of course, but opium smoking was fading as a recreational drug of choice.

Opium would be replaced by other drugs—heroin and cocaine and marijuana—but Ewen McLean didn't live to experience any of that, of course. He saw some of the changes in Hong Kong, where in 1919, the crown colony finally stopped transshipping Indian opium into China after seventy-seven years. The local monopoly still sold opium to the 400,000 smokers in the colony, so he could have picked up a five-tael tin from the Hong Kong farm. Taking it back to Vancouver would mean being a smuggler again. Ewen McLean was too old, too smart, and too rich to play that game anymore.

He turned fifty-nine in 1922, hardly an old man but one with a few health issues. Too much good food and not enough exercise, the businessman's curse, and McLean left his business interests in chilly Vancouver for the warmer climate of San Diego, where his son Dudie was living. He guessed—correctly—that the *Emerald* ring indictment, now twenty-eight years old, had been long forgotten. Nobody was looking for the old smuggler anymore, and he relaxed a bit in the year he had left. On March 26, 1923, Ewen McLean died in San Diego with his wife and family nearby. It was the end of an era.

Like the former captain of his schooner, Will Whaley turned away from the sea, though he lived on islands for the rest of his life, so the break could not be final. When he left Honolulu in October 1892 with Dr. Gilbert Foote, Whaley probably had enough of his confederates' cash to last him in Asia for the rest of his life. Even the low-end estimate of $60,000 is the equivalent of at least $1,500,000 in 2021, and he was going to a country where silver American dollars were worth even more. The money held out for just under fourteen years, which turned out to be not quite a lifetime.

He started on a flamboyant note. When he arrived in Japan, he checked back into the Grand Hotel, still Yokohama's finest, staying there for several months, spending money freely and "cutting quite a figure." If he was concerned about keeping a low profile or anxious that word of his whereabouts might get back to California, he certainly didn't let any worries show. He held a lavish dinner for the officers of the SS *China*, the ship that brought him over, and then had some new clothes made, favoring the white tropical suits, Panama hats and pith helmets of Honolulu, fond reminders of the big score that paid for everything. He cast around for some business opportunities, looking into buying a hotel, and eventually settled on a saloon, opening under the name, The Office, where exiles like himself could relax in comfort and style.

A rumor circulated in May 1893 that he intended to return to Honolulu for a visit, the announcement appearing in the Honolulu newspaper on May 15. He planned to travel on the SS *Gaelic*, arriving in Honolulu on May 29, and he'd be staying at the Sans Souci Hotel on Waikiki Beach at the foot of Diamond Head. This establishment, only recently purchased, was operated by Whaley's old buddy George Lycurgus, and Whaley no doubt looked forward to a warm welcome at the casual beachside property that would host world famous author Robert Louis Stevenson on his visit to the islands later that year.

Word of Whaley's intentions got back to the boys in San Francisco, and they dispatched one of their number, Henry Chaffey, to Honolulu. Chaffey, traveling under the name Henry Brooks, arrived on the SS *Alameda* on June 30, but if he was hoping to catch Whaley, he was disappointed. The *Gaelic* came and went, and Whaley never checked in at the Sans Souci. Brooks went home at the beginning of August on the SS *City of New York*.

Safe back in Yokohama, Whaley settled into life as a saloonkeeper, an engaging and congenial host. A visitor from Hawaii, encountering him in November 1895, said they had a nice long chat about the opium business in Hawaii in which Whaley freely admitted his former role. The visitor, a former deputy customs collector who had spent a good deal of time fruitlessly pursuing *Halcyon* around the islands and trying to monitor Whaley's activities in Honolulu, was particularly interested in two questions that had vexed the customs men for some time. How had seized opium been replaced with bricks, straw and sand while in official custody? And who was responsible? Whaley, with nothing more to hide, supposedly supplied the answers, which the former customs man considered to be quite sociable of him.

Yokohama suited Whaley, and he stayed in Japan for five years, but he had always been a rambling man, or maybe the funds were starting to pinch. Other opportunities beckoned in different directions. On August 13, 1898, he reported to the American consul in the city to apply for a passport. Almost everything in the application is true, although Whaley couldn't resist taking one more shot at his pursuers. On the line that asked him to state his permanent residence and occupation, the biggest opium smuggler in American history said that he was from San Francisco and employed as a customs officer. He made one other dubious entry on the application form, stating that he needed the passport for business and intended to return to the United States in one year. In fact, he was planning to go south. The same day that Whaley signed his application form, United States forces captured Manila, effectively ending three centuries of Spanish rule in the Philippines and placing the former colony under American management.

Despite somewhat vague American promises of "eventual" independence, the Filipino people were not all thrilled to be exchanging one colonial master for another, and this reluctance kicked off a Philippine-American War that would be much longer and bloodier than the Spanish-American conflict that had just preceded it. The new unrest did not discourage thousands of Americans from traveling to the Pearl of the Orient, where William Whaley joined other businessmen, traders and adventurers in taking advantage of Manila's opportunities. He moved quickly and by October had established himself in the newly conquered city, with new partners and a couple of completely new careers. He started off by becoming the Manila agent for Schlitz Beer, which endeared itself to the American occupation forces (but deeply offended the Women's Christian Temperance Union) by shipping 216 carloads of Milwaukee's finest to Manila in celebration of Admiral Dewey's victory at Manila Bay. Whaley's main new interest, however, was show business, vaudeville to be exact, as he encountered a former Hawaii resident and friend from the opium trade who was already in that line.

We last saw Tommy Evans in Honolulu, where he barely escaped doing a year at hard labor on the Reef for possession of some of the *Halcyon*'s opium. Evans had drifted down to Manila, too, opening a saloon and an ice plant with some money he'd brought from his last stop in Hong Kong. He wasn't really clear on exactly what that venture had been—something to do with pearls or investments, or both. He was supposed to be in Hong Kong as an immigration agent, sending Chinese workers to Hawaii for contract labor, but now Tommy was being careful to stay away from the crown colony, maybe until some heat died down. Tommy had brought his slightly warm, slightly soiled cash to Manila and bought the Alhambra Cafe, located at No. 64 Escolta Road, a prime address on what was known as "Manila's Queen of Streets." Evans was losing money on the place, so he transferred a major interest to an old partner, and Will Whaley was in the back in the saloon business.

Whaley had bigger plans for the Alhambra, converting it into a music hall and vaudeville theater, and he closed the deal on October 21. By the end of the year, he was booking acts, buying food and drink and arranging for stage productions that went on at the theater every night of the week, starting at 7:30 p.m. He found acts from as far away as Australia and kept the shows fresh and popular for almost three years, a happy and profitable enterprise. It seemed to be a successful one for Whaley, who once again cut a fine figure in Manila's rollicking postwar social scene.

One partner, Lewis M. Johnson, proved to be, in some ways, as big a character as Whaley himself. A soldier of fortune and man of uncertain means, Johnson made history by becoming the only American to witness the signing of the Filipino Declaration of Independence on June 12, 1898. Supposedly a representative of Admiral Dewey and the Americans, who didn't recognize the declaration or "Colonel" Johnson, he took a commission with Emilio Aguinaldo's rebel forces, serving as a staff member and "colonel of artillery." This was a big promotion; previously, he had been a mercenary soldier in a war between Peru and Chile before moving to Hawaii, where he served as armorer and sergeant major in the national guard during the brief uprising against the Hawaiian Provisional Government in January 1895. He had been selling motion picture devices and running a hotel in Shanghai before going to the Philippines, where he promoted himself to colonel and partnered with Whaley in the Alhambra. Whaley wrote to friends in Hawaii that he'd opened a couple of restaurants and was thriving and invited everyone to Manila.

The theater business prospered until July 1901, when the American administration of Manila prohibited the sale of alcoholic beverages on the Escolta. This affected many of the operations on the street, but it devastated the entertainment industry, which relied heavily on liquor sales to bring in customers. With his business vanishing, Whaley closed the theater and dissolved his partnership with Johnson. He had another business a block away in the Pasaje de Paz, a side street off the Escolta. This place, a saloon/casino/restaurant, was not subject to the alcohol ban but wasn't as attractive to the military trade that he'd enjoyed before, and he eventually moved to a new location a few blocks away, the slightly seedier Merchant's Club, on the banks of the Pasig River. There were no pretenses here; he was back in a familiar trade, the saloon business.

He didn't make a clean escape from the Alhambra, though, as Mattie Levy, the widow of a former partner, sued him and Johnson for fraud in March 1902. Levy's suit claimed that the two knew that the theater was insolvent and took advantage of her late husband when they let him invest in the business. The legal action, a charge that Whaley fleeced a helpless widow, did nothing to improve his reputation, which took another hit when the lower court ruled in Levy's favor. Under the existing law in the Philippines, this type of fraud could result in incarceration, and for the first time since the Red Eagle/Chinese return certificate case in 1887, Whaley faced prison time. Worse, this time he was looking at it in Manila's notorious Bilibid Prison, where conditions were awful enough that life expectancy for White men was shorter than the typical sentence. (In 1905, the prison's death rate was an appalling 438 per 1,000 inmates per year.) Suddenly, the Philippines didn't look so welcoming.

Whaley and Johnson spent a short stretch in Bilibid as the case continued to work its slow way through the court system, getting released as Whaley appealed, but the legal fees and the pressures took a toll. Business at the Merchants Club, with a reputation for attracting a lower-class clientele, began to suffer, and Whaley's financial problems with the lawsuit were draining him. Whaley would be forced to close this place too.

By this time, his partners had started to bail out on him. Johnson went off to start a pearl diving business elsewhere in the Philippines. Evans departed for the States, turning up in New England, where he tried to marry a wealthy young Connecticut widow. This scandalized Honolulu society, which apparently was prepared to tolerate opium selling and other misdemeanors but chided him that he'd abandoned his wife and children back in the islands, and before he sank so low as bigamy, he should at least make some provision for them. At least one local paper published a rather complete account of Evans's various misdeeds, probably hoping the widow, "barely out of her teens," would see it and wise up. She might have, as the marriage fell through, and back in the Philippines, Will Whaley was pretty much on his own.

As if all of this wasn't enough, Whaley's health began to fail. He had put on quite a bit of weight over the years, did little or no exercising and indulged in good food and plenty of alcohol. He was probably diabetic and was definitely suffering the first stages of what was then called Bright's disease—acute nephritis of the kidneys. This was the same ailment that had killed his former acquaintance from Hawaii King David Kalākaua in January 1891. The symptoms include bloating and swelling, so Whaley put more weight on his five-foot-eleven frame. Kidney stones and back and testicular pain, mild at first but all chronic, led him into laudanum's arms, if not those of morphine and heroin as well. These were all available on a doctor's prescription in 1905 Manila and without a prescription in patent medicines, so long as the label listed the active ingredients. Until 1907, an opium smoker could get a pipe full in Manila, too, as a licensed monopoly serviced a trade that had been ongoing in the islands for over one hundred years and didn't stop when the Americans came. Maybe Will Whaley went down that road to ease a few pains, getting a close look at his old business from a new perspective.

He got a little good news in 1905, when the Supreme Court of the Philippines ruled that there had been no fraud and dismissed the Levy lawsuit against him. No longer facing a prison term, he took jobs as a common laborer, even working as a "dock walloper," loading and unloading the merchant vessels that brought war supplies and trade goods to America's newest overseas colony. But his health waned, and early in 1907, he applied to the American government for permission to be transported to the United States. Will Whaley declared himself an indigent, asking to be taken home at government expense. The money he had gotten from the biggest opium deal in American history, at least $100,000 in cash, $2.7 million in 2021 dollars, was all gone. It had lasted the King of the Opium Ring a little under fifteen years.

Burial at sea aboard the U.S. Army Transport *Thomas*. Will Whaley's final resting place. San Francisco Chronicle.

While he waited for the Army's Quartermaster Corps' approval, his condition worsened, and Whaley checked into Manila's St. Paul's Hospital, remaining there for thirty-nine days until word came that he would be taken aboard the United States Army Transport *Thomas*, sailing for Honolulu and San Francisco. Even today, the treatment for Bright's disease is limited, and the prognosis for someone in Whaley's condition is grim. He told people that he hoped to recover his health at home in California but though he had crossed this same ocean many times before in the first-class cabins of the most luxurious steamships on the Pacific, he spent this voyage in the *Thomas*'s sick bay, too ill to go on deck. The transport tried out its new toy, a wireless radio that put the ship in touch with shore stations around the world, and Whaley faded as the ship cruised north and east, heading into the waters near Hawaii, where his beautiful schooner once hovered, waiting for the chance to deliver its cargo.

On July 28, 1907, the logbook of the USAT *Thomas* recorded that W.A. Whaley, a civilian employee, died at sea. The ship was still a couple of days out of Honolulu, and the crew transferred him from the sick bay into the hold. Their orders were to deliver the indigent citizen to California. The ship stopped in Honolulu and then continued on to San Francisco, arriving there at last on August 14. After sixteen years away, and almost twenty years to the day after *Halcyon* set sail for its first opium cruise, Will Whaley had come home. A former shipmate, selling his story to the newspapers under the assumed name of "Captain Felix," got many of the details of Whaley's story right and a few major ones wrong. He said Whaley carried opium from Victoria to Hawaii, and that never happened. He said *Halcyon* stopped in Honolulu, and there is no evidence it ever put in there, either. And he said Whaley was "buried at sea as an indigent" from the *Thomas*, something that the *San Francisco Chronicle*, which printed the story, played up, liking the dramatic effect and illustrating the event with a drawing.

In fact, the army's records show that it returned Whaley home as it had been ordered to do, delivering the body to "McGowan and Worley, Undertakers" in San Francisco when the *Thomas* docked on August 14. This would seem to show that William A. Whaley, "indigent citizen," was buried in his birth state of California, his grave long since lost and forgotten, as was the King of the Opium Ring himself. But George McGowan and Alfred L. Worley were a pair of San Francisco attorneys, not undertakers at all, and they might have only handled Whaley's personal effects and the details of the burial at sea as reported in the *Chronicle*, so the circumstances of the King of the Opium Ring's final resting place truly are unknown.

25

THE WITCH'S WAR IS OVER

Akutan Island, Alaska, November 11–12, 1918

Harry Tevis wouldn't have recognized his *Halcyon* at its winter mooring that November afternoon. He'd built it as a racing yacht, but now it stank of whale oil, old blood, cured salmon, seal skins and the cargoes of bone meal and building material that they'd filled it with in the years since it'd left its earlier careers. There were gasoline fumes, too, the product of a new auxiliary engine, tucked below in the space where the owner's luxurious cabin had once been. The fine staterooms were gone, along with the furnishings that had made it the marvel of the Pacific Yacht Club and the belle of the San Francisco Bay. The hull, once gleaming black, had faded to a dull, dark gray, its brightly varnished masts and topsides worn down to the bare oak. A chunky deckhouse squatted aft of the mainmast, breaking up the classic, clean lines that once made it the fastest ship ever built on America's West Coast.

All those years in the sealing and merchant trades had taken their toll, but the five after might have been worse. Now a tired thirty-five, the ship had put a half million miles in its wake (and almost ten miles on land) from Hong Kong to Hawaii to Alaska's frozen north and twenty trips to the sealing grounds of Japan and Russia. It'd had a half dozen different careers, two different names and six owners, and it was played out. On Armistice Day, it strained against its chains as the night closed in and the winds increased.

Its sealing career ended in 1913, when government bans on pelagic sealing all but eliminated the business, and *Vera* changed ownership again. Rumor had it being transferred to a Canadian group that was planning an Arctic expedition, but these plans fell through. Instead, it went to an American fishing concern, a Seattle-based group, the North Pacific Fisheries Company, which planned to mild cure salmon at Forester Island, Alaska. The Canadian registry closed on December 31, 1914, as the new owners gave the ship the old name back, reregistering it under the American flag as *Halcyon*. It collected its old registry number, 95914, but did not remain in the company's hands for long. By 1915, it had been sold again, this time to Edward M. Peterson and brothers John and Thomas Tjerandsen, who planned to use it to haul cargo between Seattle and Mexico or Alaska. They also gave *Halcyon* an important upgrade, installing the gasoline engine, which changed its classification from a sailing ship to a power schooner.

Truthfully, the ship was a failure in its latest role, one that didn't call for either the speed of a racer or the luxury of a yacht. It simply didn't have the size to profitably haul anything other than high-value cargoes, certainly not salmon or building materials, though its previous owner had tried gamely to make it work as a power freighter on the Inside Passage between Seattle and Southeastern Alaska. A year earlier, they gave it up and sought a buyer. They found one with North Pacific Sea Products Company, a Seattle-based firm that operated whaling stations in the Aleutian Islands. *Halcyon* serviced the station and the small fleet of harpoon ships based at Akutan Island for the season that ended in the fall of 1918. But the ships it tended had gone south, and the crew of twelve was all ashore that evening in November 1918, leaving little *Halcyon* alone in the harbor to face the tempest as the rest of the world greeted peace.

By midnight, the men at Akutan knew this wasn't just an ordinary Alaska winter storm. Before dawn, there was some praying going on. Sometime in the early morning hours, the hurricane-force wind tore roofs from buildings and ripped away walls, doing over $5,000 in damage to the whaling station. Visibility closed to a matter of feet, making it dangerous to go outside with driving snow and absolute darkness concealing everything beyond the pools of light that spilled from the windows of each occupied building. Although they were only yards from the water's edge, the crew could see nothing of the anchorage, where the wind shredded the surface of the icy water, driving the spray in long sheets along the shore toward the open mouth of the bay and scouring the little ship.

Last known photograph of Halcyon, after its conversion to a power schooner. *Family of Thomas and Jack Tjerandsen.*

With the gale still howling at first light, a pale gray dawn broke over an empty harbor. *Halcyon* had disappeared, far from the first time that the little schooner had vanished into the vast Pacific. Tom Williamson, the foreman, reported the casualty to the Coast Guard. "Severe SW storm towards evening and very dark.…Vessel was laid up at mooring for winter, had two anchors down, no one on board. Vessel must have broken anchor chains.…Unable to do anything as no vessel was available to assist and weather was too bad for the small boat we had." Although he hadn't seen the ship go and he didn't know what exactly had happened to it, Williamson gave his bleak estimate of *Halcyon*'s chances in the storm of the season: "Total loss."

As it had done so many times before, *Halcyon* vanished, this time into history. No one knows what became of it that long night in November 1918. It might have crossed Akun Pass, struck Akun Island and gone down along that rocky shore, but no wreckage was ever found. It might have kept sailing on that big southwest wind, ridden it on toward the Alaska coast or the Bering Strait, but no trace of it was ever seen again. Maybe it holed itself on a rock, going down in deep water, becoming another of Alaska's many lost ships, vanishing without a trace in the Great North's icy and treacherous winter waters. Perhaps it's in the shallows somewhere on the coastline, waiting for someone to find it well preserved by the cold, one thousand stories in the wreck.

Or maybe the legendary *Halcyon*, the most notorious of the opium runners and fastest sailing ship ever built on the West Coast is out there still. It's fitting that its end should be a mystery, as was so much of its life.

BIBLIOGRAPHY

Adams, Samuel Hopkins. *The Great American Fraud: A Series of Articles on the Patent Medicine Evil, Reprinted from Collier's Weekly*. New York: P.F. Collier and Sons, 1905.

Adler, Jacob. "The Hawaiian Navy under Kalākaua." *Seventy-Third Annual Report of the Hawaiian Historical Society, for the Year 1964* (1965): 7–22.

Adler, Jacob, and Gwynn Barrett. *The Diaries of Walter Murray Gibson, 1886, 1887*. Honolulu: University Press of Hawai'i, 1973.

"The Age of Drugs." *Puck Magazine* 48, no. 1231 (October 10, 1900).

American Medical Association. *Nostrums and Quackery*. Chicago: Press of American Medical Association, 1912.

An Act to Amend an Act Entitled "An Act to Establish a Penal Code," Approved February 14, 1872, by Adding a New Section Thereto, to Be Known as Section 307, Relating to the Sale and Use of Opium, March 4, 1881. *Statutes of California and Amendments to the Codes, 1881, 24th Session of the Legislature* (Sacramento: State Office, 1881).

Asbury, Herbert. *The Barbary Coast: An Informal History of the San Francisco Underworld*. Garden City, NY: A.A. Knopf, 1933.

Baker, E.N. "The Opium Industry." *Economic Journal* 6, no. 21 (1896): 114–22.

Bell, Bob Boze. *The Illustrated Life and Times of Doc Holliday*. Phoenix, AZ: Tri Star-Bose, 1995.

Billing, John S., et al. *The Liquor Problem: A Summary of Investigations Conducted by the Committee of Fifty, 1893–1903*. Boston: Houghton Mifflin, 1905.

Blaney, Charles. *King of the Opium Ring*. New York: J.S. Ogilvie, 1905.

Board of Supervisors, San Francisco. *San Francisco Municipal Reports for the Fiscal Year 1887–1888, Ending June 30, 1888*. San Francisco: W.M. Hinton & Co., 1888.

———. *San Francisco Municipal Reports for the Fiscal Year 1888–1889, Ending June 30, 1889*. San Francisco: W.M. Hinton & Co., 1889.

———. *San Francisco Municipal Reports for the Fiscal Year Ending June 30, 1890*. San Francisco: W.M. Hinton & Co., 1890.

Boessenecker, John. *Lawman: The Life and Times of Harry Morse, 1835–1912*. Norman: University of Oklahoma Press, 1998.

Brook, Timothy, and Bob Tadashi Wakabayashi. *Opium Regimes: China, Britain, and Japan, 1839–1952*. Berkeley: University of California Press, 2000.

Brown, Giles T. *Ships That Sail No More: Marine Transportation from San Diego to Puget Sound, 1910–1940*. Lexington: University of Kentucky Press, 1966.

Chang, Hsin-Pao. *Commissioner Lin and the Opium War.* New York: W.W. Norton, 1964.

Chapin, Helen G. "The Queen's 'Greek Artillery Fire': Greek Royalists in the Hawaiian Revolution and Counterrevolution." *Hawaiian Journal of History* 15 (1981): 1–23.

Char, Tin-Yuke. *The Sandalwood Mountains: Readings and Stories of the Early Chinese in Hawai'i*. Honolulu: University Press of Hawai'i, 1975.

Char, Tin-Yuke, and Wai Jane Char. "The First Chinese Contract Laborers in Hawaii, 1852." *Hawaiian Journal of History* 9 (1975): 128–35.

Clemens, Samuel (Mark Twain). *Roughing It*. Vol. 1. New York: Harper & Brothers Publishers, 1899.

Coman, Katharine. "The History of Contract Labor in the Hawaiian Islands." *Publications of the American Economic Association* 3rd series 4, no. 3 (August 1903): 1–61.

Coolidge, Mary Roberts. *Chinese Immigration*. New York: Henry Holt, 1909.

Corran, W.H.L., comp. *Langley's San Francisco Directory for the Year Commencing April 1880 (et seq): Accurate Index of Residents and a Business Directory; Also, a Guide to Streets, Public Offices, Etc. and a Reliable Map of the City*. San Francisco: Francis, Valentine & Co., 1880–95.

Courtwright, David T. *Dark Paradise: A History of Opiate Addiction in America*. Cambridge, MA: Harvard University Press, 2009.

Crocker, H.S., comp. *Crocker-Langley San Francisco Directory*. San Francisco: H.S. Crocker Company, 1896–1907.

Dalton, Anthony. *The Graveyard of the Pacific: Shipwreck Tales from the Depths of History*. Victoria, BC: Heritage House Publishing, 2010.

Davidson, Lance S. "Shanghaiied!: The Systematic Kidnapping of Sailors in Early San Francisco." *64 California History 1* (Winter 1985): 10:17.

Dill, John Gordon. "On the Use of Modified Opium Smoking in Pulmonary Tuberculosis." *Lancet*, July 11, 1891.

Dillon, Richard H. *The Hatchet Men: San Francisco's Brotherhood of Blood.* Sausalito, CA: Comstock Editions, 1962.

Druggists' Circular and Chemical Gazette. Vol. 32. N.p.: Oil, Paint and Drug Publishing, 1888.

Dubos, Rene Jules, and Jean Dubos. *The White Plague: Tuberculosis, Man, and Society*. New Brunswick, NJ: Rutgers University Press, 1952.

Dye, Bob. *Merchant Prince of the Sandalwood Mountains: Afong and the Chinese of Hawaii.* Honolulu: University of Hawai'i Press, 1997.

Dye, Robert Paul. "Merchant Prince: Chun Afong in Hawaii, 1849–90." *Journal of the Chinese Historical Society of America, The Hawaii Chinese* (2010): 23–36.

Eckenrode, Hamilton James, and Pocahontas Wilson Wight. *Rutherford B. Hayes: Statesman of Reunion.* New York: Dodd, Mead & Co., 1930.

Eitel, E.J. "Supplementary Notes of the History of Hongkong, with Tables Showing Population, Income, Expenditure, Shipping from 1882–1890." *China Review* 22, no. 2 (1893–94): 532–43.

Glick, Clarence E. *Sojourners and Settlers, Chinese Migrants in Hawai'i.* Honolulu: University Press of Hawai'i, 1980.

Griffith, Sarah M. "Border Crossings: Race, Class, and Smuggling in Pacific Coast Chinese Immigrant Society." *Western Historical Quarterly* 35 (Winter 2004): 473–92.

Hart A. *Office of the Chief Medical Examiner City and County of San Francisco.* Fiscal Year 2013–14 Annual Report for FY 2010–2011, 2013.

Hay, John. *Exclusion of Chinese Laborers: Letter of Mr. John Hay, Dated December 18, 1901 [transmitting a Letter from the Chinese Minister, Washington, Dec. 10, 1901] Concerning the Exclusion of Chinese Laborers. [Together with Treaties of 1868, 1888, and 1894 Between China and the United States.* Washington, D.C.: Government Printing Office, 1901.

Hittell, John Shertzer. *The Commerce and Industries of the Pacific Coast of North America*. San Francisco: A.L Bancroft, 1882.

Inglis, Brian. *The Forbidden Game: A Social History of Drugs*. New York: Charles Scribner's Sons, 1975.

Janin, Hunt. *The India-China Opium Trade in the Nineteenth Century.* Jefferson, NC: McFarland and Company, 1999.

Kiste, Robert C. "Pre-Colonial Times." In *Tides of History: The Pacific Islands in the Twentieth Century*, by K.R. Howe, Robert C. Kiste and Brij V. Lal, 3–28. Honolulu: University of Hawai'i Press, 1994.

Kolb, Lawrence, and A.G. Du Mez. *The Prevalence and Trend of Drug Addiction in the United States, and Factors Influencing It. Treasury Department, U.S. Public Health Service, Reprint No. 924.* Washington, D.C.: U.S. Government Printing Office, 1924.

Kuykendall, Ralph S. *Foundation and Transformation, 1778–1854.* Vol. 1 of *The Hawaiian Kingdom.* Honolulu: University of Hawai'i Press, 1938.

———. *The Kalākaua Dynasty, 1874–1893.* Vol. 3 of *The Hawaiian Kingdom.* Honolulu: University of Hawai'i Press, 1967.

Lai, David Chuenyan. *Chinatowns: Towns Within Cities in Canada.* Vancouver: University of British Columbia Press, 1988.

Levi, Steven C. *Boom and Bust in the Alaska Goldfields: A Multicultural Adventure.* Westport, CT: Praeger, 2000.

Lili'uokalani. *Hawaii's Story by Hawaii's Queen.* Boston: Lothrop, Lee & Shepard, 1898.

Lim-Chong, Lilly. *Opium and the Law: Hawai'i, 1856–1900.*" Master's thesis, University of Hawaii, 1978.

Lim-Chong, Lilly, and Harry V. Ball. "Opium and the Law: Hawaii 1856–1900." *Journal of the Chinese Historical Society of America, The Hawaii Chinese* (2010).

Liu, Fu-ju. "A Comparative Demographic Study of Native-Born and Foreign-Born Chinese Populations in the United States." PhD. diss., Michigan State College, 1953.

London, Jack. *Martin Eden.* New York: McKinlay, Stone and McKenzie, 1909.

———. *The Sea Wolf.* Oxford: Oxford University Press, 2000.

———. "The Sheriff of Kona." In *House of Pride*, 193–232. New York: MacMillan, 1919.

———. *The Turtles of Tasman.* New York: Grosset & Dunlap, 1911.

Loomis, Albertine. *For Whom are the Stars?* Honolulu: University of Hawai'i Press, 1976.

———. "The Longest Legislature." *Seventy-First Annual Report of the Hawaiian Historical Society for the Year 1962* (1963): 7–27.

Lubbock, Basil. *The Opium Clippers.* Glasgow, UK: Brown, Son & Ferguson, 1933.

Lucas, Jim. "The Camarinos Family of Hawaii." San Francisco Greeks. http://www.sanfranciscogreeks.com.

Manning, D. "Letter from the Secretary of the Treasury, transmitting Report of Awards of Compensation in Lieu of Moieties to Informers and Seizing Officers in Customs Fines and Forfeiture for the Fiscal Year Ended June 30, 1885." In *United States Congressional Serial Set, Volume 2387, Executive Documents of the House of Representatives, Volume 14.* Washington, D.C.: Government Printing Office, 1886.

Master carpenter certificate, by William I. Stone, for schooner Halcyon, built in 1883. May 17, 1887. National Archives and Records Administration.

Masters, Frederick J. "Opium and Its Votaries." *Californian Illustrated Magazine* 1 (October 1891 May 1892): 631–45.

"*Mattie E. Levy, administratrix of the estate of Samuel J. Levy v. L.M. Johnson, W. A. Whaley, Paul Blum and Henry* Blum. No 1786, August 12, 1905." *Reports of Cases Determined by the Supreme Court of the Philippine Islands, from April 22, 1904 to September 7, 1905, Vol. IV.* Manila: Bureau of Printing, 1907.

Maxwell's Los Angeles City Directory and Gazetteer of Southern California, 1895. Los Angeles: Los Angeles Directory Co., 1896.

McIllwain, Jeffrey Scott. *Organizing Crime in Chinatown: Race and Racketeering in New York City, 1890–1910.* Jefferson, NC: McFarland & Company, 2004.

McLean v. Hager, Collector, et al., 31 F. 602 (1887).

Miners, Norman. *Hong Kong Under Imperial Rule, 1912–1941.* Hong Kong: Oxford University Press, 1987.

Morgan, H. Wayne. *Drugs in America: A Social History, 1800–1980.* Syracuse, NY: Syracuse University Press, 1981.

———. *Yesterday's Addicts: American Society and Drug Abuse, 1865–1920.* Norman: University of Oklahoma Press, 1974.

Murphy, Kevin C. *The American Merchant Experience in Nineteenth Century Japan.* London: Routledge Curzon, 2003.

National Archives and Records Administration (NARA). Selected Indexes to Naturalization Records of the U.S. Circuit and District Counts, Northern District of California, 1852–1928. Microfilm, T1220, 1.

"National Register of Historic Places Inventory—Nomination Form." Department of the Interior, National Park Service. https://npgallery.nps.gov.

"New Pacific Coast Schooners." *Forest and Stream: A Weekly Journal of the Rod and Gun* 20 (February 1883–July 1883): 394–95.

Oliver, Harper, and Owen Davis. *The Opium Smugglers of Frisco; or, The Crimes of a Beautiful Opium Fiend, a Thrilling Drama by John Oliver.* New York: J.S. Ogilvie, 1908.

"Opium: Prepared for Smoking, and All Other Preparations of, Not Specially Provided For." *S. Rep. 53* (1895).

"Opium Smuggling." *Illustrated American* (November 7, 1891): 545.

Osorio, John K. *Dismembering Lāhui: A History of the Hawaiian Nation to 1887.* Honolulu: University of Hawai'i Press, 2002.

Paint, Oil & Drug Review 5, no. 20 (October 15, 1887): 17.

Parker, Charles Wallace. *Who's Who in Western Canada: A Biographical Dictionary of Notable Men and Women in Western Canada.* Vancouver, BC: Canadian Press Association, 1911.

Passenger Lists, 1865–1935. Department of Employment and Immigration fonds. Library and Archives Canada Ottawa, ON. Microfilm T-479 to T-520, T-4689 to T-4874, T-14700 to T-14939, C-4511 to C-4542. Library and Archives Canada, n.d. RG 76-C.

Patterson, T.W. *Hellship!* Langley, BC: Stagecoach Publishing, 1974.

People v. Northey, 77 Cal., 618 (1887).

Potash, Steve. "Pacific Mail Steamship Company: Historical Essay." Shaping San Francisco's Digital Archive, http://www.foundsf.org.

Prince, Carl E., and Mollie Keller. *The U.S. Customs Service: A Bicentennial History.* Washington, D.C.: Department of the Treasury, 1989.

Pure Food and Drug Act Hearings Before the House Comm. on Interstate and Foreign Commerce, House of Representatives, Sixty-Second Congress, Second Session. (1912).

Register of Officers and Agents, Civil, Military, and Naval, in the Service of the United States. Washington, D.C.: Government Printing Office, series 1865–1900.

Register of Officers and Agents, Civil, Military, and Naval, in the Service of the United States, on the Thirtieth of September 1875. Washington, D.C.: Government Printing Office, 1876.

Report of the Joint Special Comm. to Investigate Chinese Immigration. (February 27, 1877).

"Report of the League of Nations Advisory Committee on Traffic in Opium, May 1937." In *Majority Judgment of the Tokyo International Military Tribunal* 102, 49, 326.

Salaries of Customs and Internal Revenue Officers: Hearing Before the House Comm. on Ways and Means, Sixtieth Congress, First Session. (1908).

Sanderson, J. *An Ocean Cruise and Deep Water Regatta of the Pacific Yacht Club, July, 1884.* San Francisco: H.S. Crocker & Co., 1884.

Savage, Richard Henry. *The Flying Halcyon: A Mystery of the Pacific Ocean.* London: George Routledge and Sons, 1894.

Scholefield, Ethelbert Olaf Stuart. *British Columbia from the Earliest Times to the Present.* Vol. 4. Vancouver, BC: S.J. Clarke Publishing Co., 1914

Silver, Gary, ed. *The Dope Chronicles, 1850–1950.* New York: Harper, 1979.

Sinn, Elisabeth. "Preparing Opium for America: Hong Kong and Cultural Consumption in the Chinese Diaspora." *Journal of Chinese Overseas* 1, no. 1 (2005): 16–42.

Soennichsen, John Robert. *The Chinese Exclusion Act of 1882*. Santa Barbara, CA: Greenwood, ABC-CLIO, 2011.

Sweeting, A.E. *Education in Hong Kong, Pre-1841 to 1941: Fact and Opinion*. Hong Kong: Hong Kong University Press, 1990.

"T. Williamson, U.S. Customs Report of Casualty, November 15, 1918." In *Alaska Shipwrecks: 1750–2010, by* Warren Good. www.alaskashipwrecks.com.

Taylor, Albert Pierce. "The Golden Wallet of Fate." *Paradise of the Pacific* 40, no. 1 (January 1927).

Three Thousand Eight Hundred and Eighty Boxes of Opium v. United States, 23 Fed. 367 (1883).

Thurston, Lorrin A. *Memoirs of the Hawaiian Revolution*. Honolulu, HI: Advertiser Publishing, 1936.

Travers, Harold H. "Colonial Relations and Opium Control Policy." In *Drugs, Law, and the State*, by Harold H. Travers and Mark S. Gaylord. Hong Kong: Hong Kong University Press, 1992.

Tsai, Shih Shan Henry. *The Chinese Experience in America*. Bloomington: Indiana University Press, 1986.

Tu, Tsungming. "Statistical Studies on the Mortality Rates and the Causes of Death among the Opium Addicts in Formosa." *United Nations Bulletin on Narcotics* (January 1, 1951): 9–11.

Twentieth Annual List of Merchant Vessels of the United States. Washington, D.C.: Government Printing Office, 1889.

United States Comptroller of the Treasury. *Decisions of the Comptroller of the Treasury*. Vol. 14. Washington, D.C.: Government Printing Office, 1908.

United States Department of Commerce. *Report of the United States Commissioner of Fisheries for the Fiscal Year 1918*. Washington, D.C.: Government Printing Office, 1920.

United States Department of State. Despatches, Honolulu, Hawaiʻi and Kanagawa, Japan. Microfilm. 1886–95.

United States Department of State. *Papers Relating to the Foreign Relations of the United States*. Washington, D.C.: Government Printing Office, 1918.

United States Department of the Treasury, Bureau of Internal Revenue. *Internal Revenue Laws in Force May 1, 1920*. Washington, D.C.: Government Printing Office, 1920.

Vinnedge, Dale. *Alaska's Whaling Coast*. Charleston, SC: Arcadia Publishing, 2013.

Voss, John Claus. *The Venturesome Voyages of Captain Voss.* New York: Dodd, Mead & Co., 1941.

The Western Druggist, A Journal of Pharmacy, Chemistry, and Allied Sciences. Vol. 9. Chicago: G.P. Englehard & Co., 1888.

Wise, John H. to the Senate, 1897, *Congressional Record: Containing the Proceedings and Debates of the Fifty-Fifth Congress, First Session, Volume XXX*. At 1,292 (May 27, 1897).

Wright, E.W., ed. *Lewis and Dryden's Marine History of the Pacific Northwest: An Illustrated Review of the Growth and Development of the Maritime Industry, from the Advent of the Earliest Navigators to the Present Time, with Sketches and Portraits of a Number of Well Known Marine Men.* Portland, OR: Lewis & Dryden Printing Company, 1895.

Yentsch, Anne E. "Tracing Immigrant Women and Their Household Possessions in 19th Century San Francisco." In *South of Market: Historical Archaeology of 3 San Francisco Neighborhoods*, edited by Mary Praetzellis and Adrian Praetzellis, 181–84. Rohnert Park, CA: Anthropological Studies Center, 2009.

Newspapers

Chicago Tribune
Daily Alta California (San Francisco)
Daily Bulletin (Honolulu)
Hawaiian Gazette (Honolulu)
Hawaiian Star (Honolulu)
Honolulu Advertiser
Independent (Honolulu)
Indianapolis News, 1900
Lima News, 1899
Los Angeles Herald
Morning Astorian (OR), 1886
Nevada State Journal (Reno), 1891
New York Herald
New York Times
Oakland Tribune
Pacific Commercial Advertiser (Honolulu)
Sacramento Record-Union
San Francisco Call
San Francisco Chronicle
Santa Cruz Sentinel
Saturday Press (Honolulu), 1883
Sausalito News, 1887
Seattle Post Intelligencer
St. Louis Post Dispatch
Vancouver Daily World
Victoria Daily Colonist
Washington Standard (Olympia)
Woodland (CA) *Daily Democrat*, 1892

ABOUT THE AUTHOR

John Madinger's law enforcement career spanned thirty-five years as a criminal investigator and narcotic agent, where he was a specialist in money laundering, asset forfeiture and financial investigations. A court-certified expert witness on money laundering, he is the author of *Money Laundering: A Guide for Criminal Investigators*, Third Edition (2011) and currently works for the Department of the Treasury providing technical assistance to foreign governments around the world. He has a bachelor of arts in criminal justice from Indiana University and an master of arts in history from the University of Hawaii.

In addition to three editions of *Money Laundering*, he is the author of *Confidential Informant: Law Enforcement's Most Valuable Tool* (1999), and his first novel, *Death on Diamond Head*, was published in 2008. The second, *Pipe Dreams*, was published in 2020. He has received awards for academic writing, novels, textbooks, short stories and poetry.